THE RISE OF ECCLESIASTICAL CONTROL IN QUEBEC

BY

WALTER ALEXANDER RIDDELL

AMS PRESS
NEW YORK

COLUMBIA UNIVERSITY
STUDIES IN THE
SOCIAL SCIENCES

174

The Series was formerly known as
Studies in History, Economics and Public Law.

Reprinted with the permission of Columbia University Press
From the edition of 1916, New York
First AMS EDITION published 1968
Manufactured in the United States of America

Library of Congress Catalogue Card Number: 75-76703

AMS PRESS, INC.
NEW YORK, N. Y. 10003

PREFACE

THIS dissertation is the outgrowth of a deep interest in those national problems in Canada which have arisen out of the historical relations between the ecclesiastical and governmental authorities in Quebec. The study was begun as a brief essay on Canadian ecclesiology, under Dr. Bayles, formerly of Columbia University. It was gradually broadened under the inspiration and suggestion of Professor Franklin H. Giddings, into the present monograph on the sociological and historical factors which led up to and made possible the control of the Roman Catholic church in Quebec.

The aim of the dissertation throughout has been to present sufficient source material to afford the general reader a basis upon which to form an adequate judgment of the sociological and historical origins in Quebec, which have been responsible in a large part for the present racial and religious situation in Canada as a whole. With this in view, the author has quoted liberally from manuscript and other source material, most of which is the result of researches in the archives of London, Paris and Ottawa. As far as possible the text has been reproduced without emendations and a literal rendering of the original French and Latin has been given.

I wish to express my thanks to those who have helped me. Especially am I grateful to Professor Franklin H. Giddings, and Professor Alvan A. Tenney, for continued interest and guidance; and to Professor Herbert L. Osgood, for criticism as to material and arrangement. I am also deeply indebted to Professor John Home Cameron, of the University of

Toronto, for invaluable help with many of the French translations and in revision and preparation of the manuscript for publication, and to David Duff, M. A., of the same institution, for assistance with the Latin translations. Among many courtesies received from librarians and archivists, my thanks are especially due to H. P. Biggar, B. Litt., English and French representative of the Canadian Archives, and to Dr. Arthur G. Doughty, and staff, for assistance in gaining personal access of the author to valuable manuscript sources in London, Paris and Ottawa; and to Miss Georgiana C. Nelles, for assistance in the preparation of the bibliography and in proof-reading.

CONTENTS

PART I

DEMOGRAPHIC AND SOCIAL CONDITIONS

CHAPTER I

CHAPTER II

PAGE

CHAPTER III

Social and Moral Solidarity

PAGE

PART II

Church and State

CHAPTER IV

The Church and State in the French Period

PAGE

CHAPTER V

Church and State Under British Rule

CHAPTER VI

PART I

DEMOGRAPHIC AND SOCIAL CONDITIONS

CHAPTER I

Introduction

The history of religious organization in Canada has as yet received little attention. Numerous contributions to the field, it is true, have appeared from time to time in the form of biographies of churchmen or denominational histories but a comprehensive history of the church in Canada has still to be written. Few, if any, countries offer a richer field for a study of certain important developments in the history of the Christian Church. Much valuable material awaits the historian and sociologist for a study of such topics as: the Jesuit and other missions among the Indians; the various struggles between the different religious orders; and between the Gallican and Papal parties within the Roman Catholic church; as well as the struggle of the church for temporal supremacy; the toleration of Roman Catholicism and the provision for separate schools under British rule; the establishment of the Church of England and state support of religious institutions; denominational unions; home and foreign missions; social service; the church and the community life; and the movement for organic church union.

Among all the problems of the church in Canada, however, there are none more interesting than that of the relation of church to state, because nearly all the others are more or less intimately related to this, probably the most fascinating of them all. There are, of course, many phases of this general problem. Naturally at different periods and in different provinces different traditions arose and the relation of church and state varied greatly. The history of church and state in Quebec is undoubtedly the most interesting of all. This interest arises, not only from the fact that in this province the British government has had to deal with a population essentially French in descent and language and Roman Catholic in religion, but also from the fact that, in the face of the decline of ecclesiastical authority among the Latin peoples of Europe, the legal status granted by the British government has resulted in giving to the hierarchy such power and control over the social, political and religious life of the people, as to make the Roman Catholic Church of Quebec without a peer among the Roman Catholic churches of the world.

Many important events occurred during the long period of struggle and adjustment between the church authorities and the representatives of the British government. The chief interest in the problem, however, lies not in these features considered as striking events but in their relation to the great social forces which conditioned the adjustment that was finally made. It is the purpose of this essay to deal with these social forces and to show their relation to the growth of the control of the church itself in Quebec.

The period covered is from the settlement of the country down to "The Constitutional Act" of 1791. This in many respects is the most important period, because by the the time the Constitutional Act was passed the basis in law had been laid for all subsequent ecclesiastical history of the Roman Catholic church in Quebec; and in consequence the interplay of the social forces which introduced the period of which that act was the climax formed an essential part of the conditions which determined the entire subsequent development of religious organization in Quebec. This study, therefore, has been entitled "The Rise of Ecclesiastical Control in Quebec." Its aim is to indicate, from a sociological point of view, how closely related was the rise of that control and the social solidarity upon which it was based to the great demographic and social facts of this province. The study reviews the facts which show how inevitably the population became homogeneous, and how, for this reason there developed a social solidarity which was highly favorable for the development of a centralized and paternalistic ecclesiastical control. The character of the subjects treated is indicated by the chapter headings. In Chapter II entitled, "Demographic Factors Affecting the Homogeneity of the Population of the Province of Quebec," the attempt has been made to show how the situation of Quebec and the facts of the aggregation and composition of the population were all remarkably conducive to the production of that social and moral solidarity which the Roman Catholic church in Quebec has found so well adapted to its purposes. In Chapter III entitled, "Social and Moral Solidarity," the facts of occupation, language and other social characteristics of the population are so treated as to indicate their influence upon the same fundamental social process, namely, the production of mental and moral solidarity.

In the later chapters, the relations of the state and church are considered from a more historical standpoint but in such a way that the emphasis is still strongly upon the underlying sociological causes.

CHAPTER II

Demographic Factors Affecting the Homogeneity of the Population of the Province of Quebec

Any study of the rise of ecclesiastical control in the region now included in the Province of Quebec would be incomplete that did not recognize the strong influence of demographic and social conditions. It is these conditions which were largely responsible for the production of that homogeneous population which offered such a rich soil for the growth of ecclesiastical control.

It is the purpose of this and the following chapter to deal, as adequately as possible, with these underlying forces both demographic and social. The present chapter will deal with the first of these topics, namely, the demographic factors which affected the homogeneity of the population of Quebec, while the following chapter will deal with the social aspects of that homogeneity. The demographic facts can be treated logically, under the headings, situation, aggregation, demotic composition and demotic unity.

The situation, including the natural features, artificial features and the possible sources of subsistence of the area under consideration, was remarkably conducive to that homogeneity of population to which reference has already been made.

Among the natural features of situation the chief factor which made for homogeneity was the magnificent system of waterways. In Quebec alone the 187 principal rivers had a combined length of 13,883 miles.[1] A large part of

[1] *Quebec Statistical Year Book 1914*, pp. 46-53.

this distance was navigable by canoe and a very considerable proportion of it by larger boats. Thus the rivers provided an easy means of access to the new settlements and of escape in the event of an Indian attack. The accessibility of the territory, however, reacted most peculiarly upon its settlement and character. The rivers produced both a scattering and a concentration of population. The population became scattered because very many small settlements were formed. It was concentrated in that for the most part it did not extend back far from the banks of the rivers.

The habitat of the French Canadian, during the period from 1625-1791, was roughly coterminous with the territory later known as Lower Canada.[1] The actual settlements, however, covered only those districts in the immediate vicinity of the St. Lawrence river and its tributaries.[2] Settle-

[1] The territory comprising the province of Lower Canada by Imperial Act of 1791 was intended to include practically all the settlements of the French Canadians, and therefore may be taken as the population-area under consideration. The boundaries of the province were formed by the territory of the Hudson's Bay or East Maine on the north; the Gulf of St. Lawrence, the St. John River and the narrow strip of the Labrador coast on the east; the province of New Brunswick, the district of Maine, the province of New Hampshire, and the states of Vermont and New York on the south; and, on the west, the province of Upper Canada, the Ottawa River, Lake Temiscaming, and a line drawn due north from the head of this lake to Hudson's Bay. (Bouchette, *A Topographical Description of the Province of Lower Canada*, 1815, pp. 1-3.)

[2] "The shores are closely inhabited for about three-quarters of an English mile up the country; but beyond that the woods and the wilderness increase. All the rivulets falling into the river St. Lawrence are likewise well inhabited on both sides. I observed throughout Canada that the cultivated lands lie only along the river St. Lawrence and the other rivers in the country, the environs of towns excepted, round which the country is all cultivated and inhabited within the distance of twelve or eighteen English miles. The great islands in the river are likewise inhabited." (Kalm, *Travels into North America*, vol. iii, pp. 90-91.)

ment, almost from the first, had been widely dispersed. As early as 1667 there were enumerated in the census returns, as reaching from the city of Quebec on the east to Montreal on the west, no fewer than nineteen small communities, the largest of which had a population of only 667. By 1739 the number of settlements had increased to 137, and extended from St. Barnabé ou Rimouski on the east, to Soulanges on the west, a distance of more than 350 miles.

The seigniorial system of land tenure, also, was largely responsible for both this scattering and concentration. The desire of seigniors to obtain large tracts of land with a river frontage, induced them to push the frontier further and further away from the leading settlements. Three seigniories had been granted before 1627, namely, those of Louis Hébert in 1623, of Guillaume de Caën in 1624, and of the "Reverend Fathers of the Society and Company of Jesus" in 1626.[1] The Company of One Hundred Associates were given the right in 1627, "to improve and to settle the said lands, as they may consider to be necessary, and to distribute the same to those who will live in the said country, and to others, in such quantities and in such a manner as they shall judge proper."[2] During the Company's rule probably not more than a score of the sixty seigniories granted were given to actual settlers[3] (such as Robert Giffard), who were prepared to develop their holdings.[4]

In 1685 the number of seigniories had increased to sixty-four,[5] and in 1712 to at least ninety.[6] For a time after the

[1] Munro, William Bennett, *The Seigniorial System in Canada*, p. 21.

[2] *Edits et Ordonnances Royaux* (1803), vol. i, p. 4.

[3] Munro, *op. cit.*, p. 25.

[4] *The Jesuit Relations and Allied Documents*, 1636, vol. ix, p. 155.

[5] *Census of Canada*, 1870-1871, vol. iv, *re* Census 1685.

[6] Catalogne's Report, in Munro, *Documents Relating to the Seigniorial Tenure in Canada*, The Publications of the Champlain Society, pp. 94-151.

arrêts of Marly, fewer grants were made, and in 1719 they were refused altogether;[1] but from 1731 to the end of the French period, grants again became quite numerous.

In many cases little care was taken to secure suitable seigniors. So unsuccessful and indifferent had been many of the early seigniors, that in 1663 a decree was passed revoking all concessions remaining uncleared after a period of six months, on the ground, that

large tracts of land have been granted to all the inhabitants of the colony, who have never been in a position to clear them, and who have placed their homes in the middle of the said lands. The result has been that they are scattered about at considerable distances from one another, and are neither able to render help or assistance, nor to be assisted by the officers and soldiers of the garrisons at Quebec, and other strongholds of the said country; and moreover, it appears that in a large part of the country, only small fields lying around the dwellings of grantees have been cleared, the rest is beyond their power to clear.[2]

The lands reverting to the crown were then to be opened for settlement, by *habitants* and by new settlers in the colony.[3]

So unsatisfactory had been the company's policy in grant-

[1] *Canadian Archives*, series B. 40, (transcript from *Archives Des Colonies*), pp. 245-248; *cf.* Munro, *op. cit.*, pp. 160-162.

[2] *Edits et Ord.* (1803), vol. i, p. 24. *Cf.* "It is necessary, then, to attend to the interior of the Colony, which is in such a terrible state of disorder that no good is to be expected from it, unless it be reconstructed. This cannot be effected without causing most of the settlements to be abandoned, each seigniory being two or three leagues front, and the most populous of them having only thirty or forty settlers; the majority of them twelve to fifteen, and even five or six." (Denonville to Seignelay, 12 June, 1686, *Colonial Documents, New York*, vol. ix, p. 294; *cf. ibid.*, p. 307.)

[3] *Edits et Ord.* (1803), vol. i, p. 25.

ing seigniories, that the right was withdrawn in 1665, and placed in the hands of the officers of the crown.[1] The new policy provided that the *intendant* should furnish seigniorial holdings to all who were willing to settle on their lands, and who were in a position to meet the expense of developing them.[2]

Still the condition of settlement in the colony seems to have been looked upon by the king as unsatisfactory. For in the two *arrêts* of July 6, 1711, he sought to overcome the evil of sparsely settled seigniories by making the holding of land dependent upon its cultivation. The seigniors, on the one hand, were brought more under the control of the crown, and compelled after a year to throw open uncleared lands for settlement,[3] on the sole condition of a ground rental (*seulement de concéder les terres à titre de redevance*).[4] Also the seigniorial dues from the new colonists were made payable directly into the hands of the receiver of the royal domain at Quebec.[5] The *habitants*, on the other hand, who did not live on their lands and cultivate them, forfeited them to the seigniorial domain.[6] This eventually facilitated settlement, as the seignior could not withhold his land for better terms from the *habitants*, nor could the *habitant* retain land for speculative purposes.[7]

Although the population in the colony was sparse, and the settlement for a long time widely scattered, many of the local communities were quite thickly settled. The long

[1] Munro, *Seigniorial System*, p. 34.

[2] *Edits et Ord.* (1806), vol. ii, pp. 128c-128h.

[3] *Jeu de fief* was peculiar to the Canadian seigniorial system, for it imposed upon the seigniors the obligation of sub-granting the lands within their seigniories.

[4] Customary dues in the neighborhood. Munro, *op. cit.*, p. 89.

[5] *Edits et Ord.* (1803), vol. i, pp. 321-322.

[6] *Ibid.*, p. 323.

[7] Munro, *Seigniorial System*, p. 43.

and narrow shape of the original holdings, and the law of inheritance were responsible in a large measure for this condition. Unlike the village type of agriculturist in France, the *habitant* preferred to live on his own land.[1] The system of land survey in New France, while allowing for this preference, at the same time permitted most of the advantages of social intercourse to be found in the village of the mother country. This system, which was first adopted in 1632, divided the land along the river into narrow farms of about four *arpents* in width by forty *arpents* in depth. The advantage of such an arrangement, as Sulte points out, "is to bring the house a few steps from the river; to permit easy access to the public road situated between the house and the river; to keep social intercourse as close as possible by the vicinity of neighbors engaged in the same occupation."[2] Later, this plan of building the houses along the common road, as the Earl of Durham remarked, "established a series of continuous villages which give the country of the seigniories the appearance of a never ending street,"[3] lent itself to inter-communication, and in a large measure overcame rural isolation.[4]

[1] "All the farms in Canada stand separate from each other, so that each farmer has his possessions entirely distinct from those of his neighbour. Each church, it is true, has a little village near it; but that consists chiefly of the parsonage, a school for the boys and girls of the place, and of the houses of tradesmen, but rarely of farm-houses; and if that was the case, yet their fields were separated. The farm-houses hereabouts are generally built all along the rising banks of the river either close to the water or at some distance from it, and about three or four *arpents* [a linear measure of about 12 rods in length, Webster's International Dictionary, 1909] from each other." (Kalm, vol. iii, p. 79.)

[2] Sulte, *Royal Society of Canada, Proceedings and Transactions*, 1905, sec. ii, p. 111; *cf.* Bouchette, *British Dominions in North America*, vol. i, p. 363.

[3] *The Report of the Earl of Durham*, p. 16.

[4] "The farmers or *censitaires* usually build their houses at 100 or 200

According to the Custom of Paris, the law of inheritance did not allow more than one-fifth of a seignior's or *habitant's* holding to be disposed of (except by actual deed of sale), to the prejudice of direct or collateral heirs. When lands were held *en seigneurie*, the oldest son had special rights of inheritance, but in the case of lands *en censive* all heirs shared equally.

The desire for each heir to share in the river frontage, soon resulted in the holdings in many settlements becoming of the narrowest dimensions, sometimes having a frontage of less than 200 feet.[1]

As has been stated above, since the houses and barns were usually situated close to the road or river, it is readily seen that what the government considered very detrimental to the economic prosperity of the colony,[2] afforded unusual opportunity for inter-communication within the local settlements.

The road and the river also brought the parish church within reach of most of the settlers. These centres of social

yards distant from the road, or sometimes nearer . . . and [the homes] in most parts have the appearance of a continued village. The origin of this injudicious distribution of land is no doubt to be traced to the social character of the Canadian peasant, who is singularly fond of neighborhood, though it is also referable to the expediency which formerly existed of concentrating as much as possible the moral and physical energies of the colony, not only with a view of mutual aid in the formation of settlements, but in order the better to be able to repel the attacks of the aborigines." (Bouchette, *op. cit.*, vol. i, p. 363.)

[1] Munro, *Seigniorial System*, p. 83.

[2] In 1744 the governor and intendant complained to the French minister that the two previous bad harvests were partly due to the attempt of a large part of the *habitants* to eke out a living on the subdivided lands of their fathers. The following year the king passed an ordinance forbidding anyone to erect a house on any farm "which shall be less than an *arpent* and a half in frontage and thirty or forty *arpents* in depth." *Édits et Ord.* (1803), vol. i, pp. 551-552; *cf.* also *C. A.*, M. 384, p. 74.

as well as religious life increased rapidly. In 1685 there were forty rural parishes, each with a resident curé, and each having on the average a population of 220.

Thus, because the territory was settled almost entirely by a single population type, namely that of the Roman Catholic French, each small community soon became comprised of persons relatively alike in descent, language and religion. There was great homogeneity of population in each local group. Inasmuch, however, as the river and seigniorial systems had led to the founding of many such local groups, at about the same period, and by the same population type, there was a remarkable similarity among the local groups. In this way it came about that although there was little inter-communication, in the early days of the colony,[1] the foundation was laid for homogeneity, and subsequent social solidarity on the scale of an entire province. When later a developed system of communication by roads was added to the increasing use of the rivers, the inter-relationships established, readily produced mental and moral solidarity throughout the whole region.

The privations and hardships incident to pioneer life in the New World also operated to create a single homogeneous type of population in New France. Natural resources were abundant but not such as to create great differences in wealth between the successful and unsuccessful. Moreover, toil of a severe sort was required to exploit the resources that existed. In consequence only the vigorous could remain

[1] This lack of communication between different parts of the colony was brought to the attention of the King in 1712 by Catalogne, the crown engineer, who proposed to overcome the difficulty by having the chief road-commissioner instructed to put forth greater effort in the construction of roads and bridges. (Catalogne's report, in Munro, *Docs. S. T.*, p. 147.) Governor Murray, just fifty years later, was also of the opinion that roads were necessary to bring the various settlements together. *Constitutional Documents*, vol. i, p. 41.

permanently. Because of a high birth rate, however, this type increased rapidly. The abundance in natural resources consisted largely of fish and game, especially in the newer settlements where they afforded a considerable part of the food supply of the pioneer and fur-trader. Considerable food supplies, however, had to be imported from France in the early years of the colony. The Company of One Hundred Associates had undertaken to provide for its settlers shelter and subsistence, during the first three years following their arrival in the colony, or to give them sufficient cleared land to enable them to become self-supporting, together with the necessary grain for the first seeding, and subsistence until the following harvest.[1] In addition to this grant of cleared land, the settlers were to receive further grants of uncleared land in such quantities, and carrying with it such titles, honors, rights and powers, as the company should deem expedient.[2] The associates who founded Montreal also agreed to make provision, not only for the settlement of forty persons on the Isle of Montreal, and to increase the number annually, but also to provide them with shelter, stock, and seed.[3]

The rigorous climate, although it shut off much of the little communication there was between the neighboring settlements, and gave the members of the local communities more leisure for social intercourse, nevertheless, was of much less disadvantage to agriculture than was generally supposed. In a letter of the year 1627, Lalemant, writes in this regard that,

[1] *Edits et Ord.* (1803), vol. i, p. 3; *cf.* also Charlevoix, P. F. X., *History and General Description of New France*, trans. by Shea, vol. ii, p. 37.

[2] *Ibid.*, vol. ii, p. 40.

[3] *Archives du séminaire de Saint-Sulpice de Paris,* cited by Faillon, *Histoire de la colonie française en Canada*, vol. i, pp. 401-403.

the long duration of the snow might cause one to somewhat doubt whether wheat or rye would grow well in this country. But I have seen some as beautiful as that produced in your France, and even that which we have planted here yields to it in nothing . . . rye and oats grow here the best in the world, the grain being larger and more abundant than in France. Our peas are so beautiful; it is wonderful to see them. The further up the river we go, the more we see of the fertility of the soil.[1]

In the Jesuit Relation of 1642 is contained a similar favorable report on the agricultural possibilities:

The cereals have proved very successful; some residents now harvest more than they require for the food of their families and of their cattle, which thrive very well in this country. The time will come when all will have food.[2]

The observations of Kalm, the botanist, are especially valuable. In describing the district known as La Prairie to the south of the St. Lawrence, on his visit in 1749, he writes

The prospect is very fine . . . and as far as I could see the country, it was cultivated; all the fields were covered with corn, and they generally use summer-wheat here. The ground is still very fertile, so that there is no occasion for leaving it lie fallow . . . and in a word this country was, in my opinion the finest in North America which I had hitherto seen.[3]

In another place he writes:

The high meadows in Canada are excellent, and by far preferable to the meadows round Philadelphia and in the other

[1] *Rel.* 1616-1629, vol. iv, pp. 193-194.

[2] *Rel.* 1642, vol. xxii, pp. 39-41.

[3] Kalm, *op. cit.*, vol. iii, pp. 51-52.

English colonies. The further I advanced northward here, the finer were the meadows and the turf on them was better and closer.[1]

With regard to the yield of grain crops, Kalm states that,

wheat is the kind of corn which is sown in the greatest quantities here. The soil is pretty fertile, and they have sometimes got twenty-four or twenty-six bushels from one, though the harvest is generally ten or twelve fold. They sow likewise a great quantity of peas, which yield a greater increase than any corn; and there are examples of its producing a hundred fold.[2]

His description shows that in the district between Montreal and Three Rivers, the rich alluvial soil of the St. Lawrence valley was becoming somewhat run-out under the crude methods of agriculture. He says, "the soil is reckoned pretty fertile; and wheat yields nine or ten grains from one. But when this old man was a boy [referring to a farmer he had interviewed], and the country was new and rich everywhere, they could get twenty or four-and-twenty, grains from one." [3]

Notwithstanding the crude methods of agriculture, the struggle for subsistence, once the land was cleared, does not appear to have been difficult. The Earl of Durham speaks of the French Canadians as "occupying portions of the wholly unappropriated soil, sufficient to provide each family with material comforts, far beyond their ancient means, or almost their conceptions." [4] As early as 1636, Le Jeune, in answer to the question, "The land being cleared and ploughed, will it produce enough for the inhabitants?" wrote that it would, and cited the case of one Giffard, who from

[1] Kalm, *op. cit.*, vol. iii, p. 156.
[2] *Ibid.*, p. 206.
[3] *Ibid.*, p. 259.
[4] Durham, p. 16.

his first clearing had harvested, "eight puncheons of wheat, two puncheons of peas, and three puncheons of Indian corn"; and from the second crop he hoped to harvest enough, if his wheat yielded in proportion to indications, "to maintain twenty persons." This land had all been cleared, seeded and harvested with the help of seven men,[1] showing that even under pioneer conditions a living might be had from the soil.

As the land was heavily timbered, however, the clearing of it was a slow, difficult, and expensive process. An *arpent* and a half [about an acre and a quarter] was considered a fair year's work for one man;[2] and, as is the case in all such pioneer communities, only the more industrious and persevering could hope to succeed.

Most writers agree that the *habitants* had little difficulty in getting a living from the soil and this can doubtless be accounted for, in large measure, by their standard of living. Although considerably above that of the European peasantry, this standard consisted merely in a plentiful supply of plain food and other necessaries. Le Jeune describes a labourer's rations while clearing land as consisting of,

> two loaves of bread, of about six or seven pounds, a week,—that is a puncheon of flour a year; two pounds of lard, two ounces of butter, a little measure of oil and of vinegar; a little dried codfish, that is, about a pound; a bowlful of peas, which is about a *chopin* (pint),—and all this for one week. As to their drinks, they are given a *chopin* of cider per day, or a quart of beer, and occasionally a drink of wine, as on fête-days.

[1] *Rel.* 1636, vol. ix, p. 153.

[2] "Twenty men will clear in one year thirty *arpents* of land so clean that the plow can pass through it. . . . The usual task for one man is an *arpent* [a measure equal to .871 acres, *Quebec Statistical Year Book, 1914*, p. 199] and a half a year if he is not engaged in other work." (*Rel.* 1636, vol. ix, pp. 155-157.)

In the winter they are given a drop of brandy in the morning, if one has any. What they get from the country in hunting or fishing, is not included in this.[1]

These rations for a labourer, considering the amount of game and fish that must have been available, indicate for the whole population, in the matter of food, a fair standard of living.[2]

Whether there was any marked rise in the standard of living during the latter part of the French period seems doubtful. Occasionally, owing to a poor harvest,[3] or as the result of war,[4] we find that numbers of the population were reduced to actual want. The high price of the commodities which were not produced in the country, for a time at least, seems to have stood in the way of raising the *habitant's* standard of living. Kalm points out that

The common people in the country, seem to be very poor. They have the necessaries of life, and but little else. They are content with meals of dry bread and water, bringing all other provisions, such as butter, cheese, flesh, poultry, eggs, &c. to town, in order to get money for them, for which they buy clothes and brandy for themselves, and dresses for their women.[5]

This would seem to indicate that commodities which were produced by the inhabitants of Quebec were fairly plentiful and cheap but that few could afford to pay the high prices necessary to obtain other things. The standard of living must have been relatively uniform.

[1] *Rel.* 1636, vol. ix, p. 157; *cf. Colon Docs., N. Y.*, vol. ix, pp. 151, 398.

[2] Munro, *Docs. S. T.*, p. xciii.

[3] *Edits et Ord.* (1803), vol. i, pp. 551-552.

[4] "Thus the harvest was gathered with great tranquility, the crop was abundant, and the famine, which had begun to be felt keenly, ceased at once." (Charlevoix, vol. iv, p. 241; *cf.* also *Const. Docs.*, vol. i, p. 60.)

[5] Kalm, *op. cit.*, vol. iii, p. 192.

With the return of peace under the British rule, a large measure of prosperity was felt among the *habitants*.[1] The prospect of a comfortable house on the land became more attractive to the young men than the lure of the fur trade, so that it was said,

> nearly all Canadians—many of whom are young—build new habitations for themselves and are presented by their parents with cattle and articles for housekeeping. "Be fruitful and multiply" seems to be their motto, for the family of the new *habitant* soon begins to increase. He has however to work hard and live economically for a number of years before he is able to fill his barns with grain and enlarge his stock.[2]

Whatever weight we give to the more glowing accounts of New France, this stands out, that although resources were abundant, nevertheless the conditions of life were hard, and only the industrious and persevering could hope to exploit the environment successfully. Complaint was sometimes made that many of the early colonists were shiftless and indifferent, but this process of selection of necessity gradually developed a remarkably homogeneous type of population, thrifty and self-satisfied, traditionalistic and conservative in the extreme.

In considering the population of New France in the early days, the presence of the Indians must not be left out of account. At first thought one might assume that their presence would have tended to destroy the essential homogeneity of the population. This was not the fact,

[1] "The spirit which took possession of the towns soon spread into the most distant parts of the country, and introduced among their countrymen ideas of greater luxury and enjoyment than they had originally entertained." (*A Political and Historical Account of Lower Canada*, London, 1830, p. 117.)

[2] *Revolutionary Letters*, pp. 27-28.

however, because in reality the Indians never became an integral part of the local community, nevertheless the status of the Indians must be reviewed briefly, because of the indirect effect which their presence had upon the rise of ecclesiastical control. This indirect effect was seen in the policies of the church and government authorities with respect to the Indians which of necessity strengthened the control of the church.

At the coming of the French to the St. Lawrence valley it was the rich habitat of native races. These comprised the Algonquin and Huron-Iroquois stocks, which were divided into numerous tribes. The Huron-Iroquois were much more virile and interesting than the representatives of the great Algonquin stock,[1] and it was with these that the French had most to do. The facility with which the French were able to mingle with the Indians,[2] together with the influence of the Catholic Missions,[3] soon brought the French into more or less intimate relations with these tribes.

The success of these efforts at first led the authorities to believe that the Indians would soon adopt a Christian civilization, and as they became assimilated with the French they would be a source of strength to the population in the colony. The missionaries were to be the chief recruiting agents in this plan of collecting the Christian Indians in villages.[4]

[1] *Rel.*, vol. i, pp. 10-11.

[2] Parkman, *The Jesuits in North America*, vol. i, p. 131.

[3] These included the Montagnais, the Quebec, the Montreal, the Huron, the Iroquois and the Ottawa missions. (*Rel.*, vol. i, pp. 15-35.)

[4] "The foundations of French dominion were to be laid deep in the heart and conscience of the savage. His stubborn neck was to be subdued to the 'yoke of the Faith.' The power of the priest established, that of the temporal ruler was secure. These sanguinary hordes, weaned from intestine strife, were to unite in a common allegiance to God and the King. Mingled with French traders and French settlers, softened by French manners, guided by French priests, ruled by French

The Marquis de Seignelay, in the census of 1685 noted that,

. . . it is desirable that the colony should increase every year, not only by the addition of French but also of Indians, who should be attracted as much as possible to live among the French, as after their children shall have been accustomed to our manners, and shall have been brought up with the French, [they] will form with them only one people.[1]

Duchesneau wrote to him,

You will perceive, my Lord, by the census of the Indians that I have taken this year, that their number is increased by two hundred and seven persons. I make bold to state to you that, amidst all the plans presented to me to attract the Indians among us and to accustom them to our manners, that from which most success may be anticipated, without fearing the inconveniences common to all the others, is to establish villages of these people in our midst.

It appears even that 'tis the best, since at the mission of the Mountain of Montreal . . . in that of the Saut de la Prairie, de la Madeleine,— . . . in those of Sillery and Loretio . . .the youth are all brought up *à la française*, except in the matter of their food and dress. . . .

. . . First those missions cannot be too much encouraged, nor too much countenance be given to the gentlemen of Saint Sulpice and the Jesuit Fathers among the Indians, inasmuch as they not only place the country in security and bring peltries hither, but greatly glorify God, and the King, as the eldest

officers, their now divided bands would become the constituents of a vast wilderness empire, which in time might span the continent. Spanish civilization crushed the Indian; English civilization scorned and neglected him; French civilization embraced and cherished him." (Parkman, *The Jesuits in North America*, vol. i, p. 131; *cf.* also Charlevoix, vol. iii, pp. 197-198, 203, and Eastman, *Church and State*, p. 117.)

[1] Marquis de Seignelay, *Census*, 1685.

son of the Church, by reason of the large number of good Christians formed there. Secondly . . . were he to order me to make, in his name, a few presents to the Indians of the Villages established among us, so as to attract a greater number of them; and were he to destine a small fund for the Indian girls who quit the Ursulines, on being educated, to fit them out and marry them, and establish Christian families through their means.

I shall not fail, my Lord, to exhort the Inhabitants to rear Indians, and shall not be discouraged giving them the example, notwithstanding three have already left me, after I had incurred considerable expense on them, because I would oblige them to learn something.[1]

Although the attempt of the French to render the Indians less migratory, resulted in a very considerable number being gathered together in villages, the anticipated success in imposing a European civilization upon the natives was, at best, only very imperfectly realized among a small remnant of these.[2] In 1680 Duchesneau estimated the number of Indians thus brought together in villages at 960.[3] The census of 1685 gives the number of Indians "established among the French" as 1538 souls,[4] and thirteen years later as 1540,[5] the largest number recorded in any of the enumerations.

[1] M. Duchesneau to M. de Seignelay, *Colon. Docs. N. Y.*, vol. ix, p. 150; *cf.* also *Rel.* 1642-1643, vol. xxiv, p. 229 *et seq.*

[2] "It was long believed that it was necessary to draw the Indians near to Frenchify them; there is every reason to acknowledge that it was a mistake. Those who have approached us have not become French, and the French who frequented them have become savages. They affect to dress and live like them." (Charlevoix, vol. iii, p. 260.)

Kalm, on his visit in 1749, wrote: "There is . . . scarce one instance of an Indian's adopting the European customs." (Kalm, *op. cit.*, vol. iii, p. 154.)

[3] Duchesneau, Nov. 13, 1680, cited in *Census* 1870-71, vol. 4, p. 14.

[4] *Census*, 1685.

[5] *Ibid.*, 1698.

This number represented only a small proportion of the total Indian population accessible to French missions at the end of the seventeenth century. While it is difficult to estimate this number, with any degree of accuracy, most probably it did not exceed 28,000.[1] Considering the magnitude of the undertaking, aiming as it did to incorporate the natives with the colonial population, and at the same time the relatively meagre resources of the colony, it is rather a creditable showing. The part the missionaries played in the scheme[2] undoubtedly helped to increase the standing of the clergy with the king and his ministers. Just how this process worked out in detail, however, will be more fully discussed in chapter IV on "The Church and State in the French Period."

[1] The censuses of the Iroquois taken in 1665 by the Jesuits, and in 1677 by Wentworth Greenhalgh, give the number of warriors as 2,340 and 2,150 respectively, which represented a population of 11,700 and 10,750. (*Census* 1870-1871, vol. 4, pp. liv-lxii.) At the time of the coming of the French the Hurons numbered about 16,000; however, the war of extermination that was waged among the different tribes of the Iroquois-Huron race brought about in 1648-1649 the almost complete extinction of the Hurons. (*Ibid.*, p. liv; *cf. Rel.*, vol. i, p. 21.) In 1736 they numbered only about 260 warriors, or 1,300 souls. (*Census* 1870-1871, vol. 4, p. lx.) The Algonquins, Abenakis, Ottawas, *etc.*, in the same year were estimated to have a total of 2,885 warriors, or a population of 14,425. On the basis of these estimates the total Indian population from which these villages were likely to draw their neophytes would be between 26,475 and 27,425. (*Ibid.*)

[2] "Concerning missions to foreign tribes, likewise, I have written something to His Holiness, and about these missions, besides, I am able to assure your Eminences that they fulfil the highest hopes of the old workers in this vineyard, the Fathers of the Society [of Jesus] and of the new secular priests, who likewise have engaged in this work, they all are worthy of being held in remembrance and in affection by your Eminences. Again a number up to six hundred of baptized persons, but in a large part of infants, have been added from the barbarians, and we hope for more if the Sacred Congregation continue to support us with its favour." (Laval to their Eminences, Sept. 30, 1669, C. A., M. 128, p. 389.

The conditions described in the foregoing pages were evidently such as to lead to a relatively simple type of population so far as the white race was concerned. The presence of the Indians did indeed produce a certain racial heterogeneity in the area under consideration, but for the problem we are dealing with, namely, the rise of ecclesiastical control, the racial heterogeneity introduced by the presence of the Indians was not of great importance. The chief effect on the church was to create the problem of how the Indians could be most readily converted to Christianity and thus be made amenable to the control of the state. The church in this endeavor became vitally interested in the relations of the civil authorities and the Indians. The representatives of the hierarchy in this manner often gained much influence with the officers of government. Although the presence of the Indians thus produced a racial heterogeneity, the net result in the church was perhaps to heighten its power; the development of ecclesiastical control which resulted from the homogeneity and consequent social solidarity of the white population was merely intensified by the relations which grew out of the presence of the Indians.

From an ethnic and religious point of view the early white population in Quebec was highly homogeneous. It was drawn almost entirely from France [1] and was composed of the few survivors of the early exploration and fur-trading expeditions to the St. Lawrence, the fur-trading company officials, the missionaries and their helpers, together with the colonists who began to come in numbers after 1632. For a time the growth of population was slow, numbering only about 375 in 1640, 600 in 1650 and 2,200 in 1663.[2] During the next few years, owing largely to immigration,

[1] Garneau, *Histoire du Canada*, vol. ii, p. 102.

[2] Sulte, *R. S. C., Trans.* 1905, sec. ii, pp. 111-112.

the population increased more rapidly, as the following table shows:

POPULATION OF QUEBEC

Year	Total population	Sexes		Married [2]			Unmarried			Percentage married [5]
		Male	Female	Male	Female	Total	Male	Female	Total	
1665....	3215 [1]	2034	1181	541	520	1061	1493	661	2154	33.
1667....	3918	2406	1512	644	652	1296	1762	860	2622	33.08
1681....	9677	5375	4302	1540	1519	3059	3835	2783	6618	31.6
1685....	10725	5897	4828	1791	1672	3463	4106	3156	7262	32.3
1688....	10303	5442	4861	1747	1741	3488	3695	3120	6815	33.85
1692....	11075	5930	5145	1850	1833	3683	4080	3312	7392	33.25
1695....	12786	6943	5843	2179	2168	4347	4764	3675	8439	34.
1698....	13815	7391	6424	2370	2277	4647	5021	4147	9168	33.63
1706....	16417	8552	7865	2896	2665	5561	5656	5200	10856	33.26
1712....	18440	9502	8938	2786	2588	5374	6716	6350	13066	29.14
1716....	20531	10377	10154	3318	3340	6658	7059	6814	13873	32,82
1720....	24434	12494	11940	4609	3782	8391	7885	8158	16391	34.34
1724....	26710	13699	13011	4787	4352	9139	8912	8659	17571	34.23
1730....	33682	17364	16318	6050	5728	11778	11314	10590	21904	34.97
1734....	37716	19049	18667	6736	6593	13329	12313	12074	24387	35.34
1737....	39970	20708	19262	7378	6804	14182	13330	12458	25788	35.48
1754....	55009 [3]	.....	......	6820	6020	12840	.....	......	38961	.....
1765....	55110 [4]	28316	26794	10922	10509	21431	17394	16285	33679	38.89
1784....	113012 [3]	54064	50759	20131	19354	39485	33933	31405	65338	.....
1790....	129311 [3]	66013	63298	19375	20569	39944	42920	39604	82524	.....

Immigration which had been stimulated by active organ-

[1] The number of families enumerated in the census of 1665 was 538; 1667, 668; 1681, 1526; and 1765, 10660.

[2] The number enumerated as married includes the widowed, also.

[3] In the census of 1754, 3208; in 1784, 8189; and in 1790, 6943 of the population are unspecified as to age, sex, and conjugal relation.

[4] This enumeration does not include the population of Montreal and Quebec, which was then estimated at 14,700 (Memorandum in *Fabrique* of Cap-Santé, cited in Census of Canada 1870-1871, vol. iv, p. xxxvi.)

[5] The census facts for the various years in the table do not admit of determination of the population of marriageable age.

izations in France [1] before 1680, began to show a marked decline, so that the French Canadian population rapidly became a genetic aggregation, that is a population produced by natural increase rather than by migration. Since then, owing largely to fecundity, the population has, on an average, about doubled every thirty years.[2] Thus it did not take long to produce a single population type.

Material exists for a fairly detailed account of the various population elements that first entered the country.

The actual settlement of the country may be said to date from the restoration of Canada to France in 1632. The Bretons who came earlier than that date, with Cartier and Roberval, as well as the sixteen men who were left by Chauvin at Tadousac in 1599, and even the twenty-five who wintered in Canada in 1608, met with such hardship that it is unlikely that any of their number were alive at this time. Probably twelve or fifteen of the younger men who came later were merged with the inhabitants who began to settle in the colony after the withdrawal of the English.[3]

The French settlers who sought homes were drawn from all parts of France. Of the 84 who came between 1632 and 1640, 46 were from Perche, Beauce, Normandy and Picardy, and the rest from Champagne, Lorraine, Brie, Poitou, etc. Subsequent immigration, down to 1663, was drawn largely from the same provinces; Perche, Normandy, Beauce, Picardy, and Anjou furnishing the larger number. In 1662-63, La Rochelle and Gascony, and the southwestern provinces, began to send settlers. During this

[1] "From 1667 till 1672 a committee was active in Paris, Rouen, La Rochelle and Quebec, to recruit men, women and young girls for Canada. This committee succeeded in effecting the immigration into Canada of about 4,000 souls." (Sulte, *R. S. C., Trans.* 1905, sec. ii, p. 114.)

[2] *Ibid.*

[3] Sulte, *R. S. C., Trans.* 1905, sec. ii, p. 102.

brief period, about 150 men with a few women came from La Rochelle, Gascony, and Poitou.

From 1640 the marriage registers are fairly complete, although they do not always give the native province of the contracting parties.[1] In the records consulted by the author the native province of the contracting parties was given in 1,807 cases. These show that, while the emigration to Canada was not of the same volume for all the provinces, it was nevertheless well distributed over the whole of France. The northwestern provinces, including Flanders, Artois, Brittany, Picardy, Normandy, Isle of France, Maine (and Perche), Orléanais, Anjou and Touraine, contributed 926 or 51.2 per cent; the southwestern, including Poitou, Berry, Gascony, and Bearn, contributed 619 or 34.3 per cent; and the eastern, including Champagne, Lorraine, Alsace, Franche-Comté, Burgundy, Nivernais, Bourbonnais, Lyonnais, Auvergne, Dauphiny, Venaissin, Provence, Languedoc, Foix, and Rousillon, 262 or 14.5 per cent.[2] The larger proportion, as might be expected, came from the provinces nearer the sea-coast. The 26 of the total of 35 provinces[3] mentioned as the birthplace of these French-born settlers, include 90 per cent of both the northwestern, and southwestern, and 53.3 per cent of the eastern provinces. While these figures show that a larger proportion came from the provinces near the sea-coast, nevertheless they make it clear that the immediate ancestors of the French Canadians were fairly representative of all parts of France.

[1] Sulte, *R. S. C., Trans.* 1905, sec. ii, p. 112; *cf. Jugements et Délibérations du Conseil Souverain*, vol. i, p. 929.

[2] *Emigration au Canada, Nouvelles Acquisitions Françaises*, 9279.

[3] Robinson, James Harvey, *An Introduction to the History of Western Europe*, map, pp. 568-569. Garneau's researches reveal an even larger number: for thirty provinces are mentioned as the birthplace of French-born settlers. These include all the northwestern, 90 per cent of the southwestern, and 73 per cent of the eastern provinces. (Garneau, vol. ii, p. 102; *cf.* Dionne, *Les Canadiens-Français: Origine des Familles*, pp. xxvii-xxxiii.)

These statistics, as well as the lists compiled by others, prove that the claim generally accepted that the French Canadians are the descendants of the Normans, is not as true as the claim that English-speaking Canadians are descendants of the English, without regard to the Scotch and Irish. Ferland's list, which he compiled from registers in Quebec, Three Rivers, and Montreal, and which is the most favorable to the Norman-ancestry theory, indicates that between 1641 and 1666 a somewhat larger proportion of immigrants came from the provinces nearer the sea-coast. Of the 339 cases considered, 210 or 61.9 per cent came from the northwestern provinces, and only 98 or 38.8 per cent from Normandy; of the remainder 104, or 30.7 per cent, came from the southwestern provinces, and 25 or 7.4 per cent from the eastern provinces. Twenty-three of the 35 provinces are mentioned. These include 90 per cent of the northwestern, 80 per cent of the southwestern, and 40 per cent of the eastern provinces.[1] The researches of Sulte, for almost the same period (1645-1666), furnish somewhat similar results. Of the 475 cases considered, 239 or 50.2 per cent were from the northwestern provinces, and only 136 or 28.6 per cent from Normandy; of the remainder 215 or 45.3 per cent were from the southwestern, and 21 or 4.5 per cent from the eastern provinces,[2] while the 1,807 cases considered above, covering a period from 1640, show that 51.2 per cent were drawn from the 10 northern provinces and only 231 or 12.2 per cent were drawn from Normandy.[3] Garneau's researches in the registers of Quebec before and during the year 1700, further substantiate the above. Of the 1,931 cases where the native province was recorded, 1,096 or 56.8 per cent were

[1] Ferland, *Cours d'Histoire du Canada*, vol. i, pp. 512-516.

[2] Sulte, *R. S. C., Trans.* 1905, sec. ii, p. 112.

[3] *Emigration au Cañada, Nouv. Acq. Fr.*, 9279.

from the northwestern provinces, of whom only 341 or 17.7 per cent were from Normandy; of the remainder 680 or 35.2 per cent were from the southwestern provinces, and 155 or 8 per cent from the eastern provinces.[1]

The average from the above four groups of statistics should be even more conclusive; showing that 54.3 per cent came from the northwestern provinces and only 17.5 per cent from Normandy; 35.5 per cent came from the southwestern and 10.2 per cent from the eastern provinces.

Thus in Canada the different racial elements of the French population found a common melting-pot. Ethnographical diversities of the Baltic, Danubian, Alpine and Mediterranean stocks,[2] which centuries had not entirely overcome in the motherland, gradually disappeared through amalgamation in Quebec. At the close of our period, 1791, the French Canadian population was a more highly homogeneous genetic aggregation than even the population of France.

A number of factors contributed to the thoroughness and rapidity which characterized amalgamation in Quebec. As has been pointed out, the earlier settlers were true pioneers, ever pushing on and spreading further and further along the St. Lawrence and its tributaries. Charlevoix observed "in clearing new land the colonists thought only of settling apart from each other, so as to be able to extend more . . . and by embracing an immense territory, compared to the scanty population contained in the colony, no one could be safe from the enemy's insults." [3]

[1] Garneau, *Histoire du Canada*, vol. ii, pp. 101-102.

[2] For the ethnological meaning of these stocks, *cf.* William Z. Ripley, *The Races of Europe*, pp. 121, 131-157, 163-179; and Franklin H. Giddings, "What Shall We Be?" *The Century Magazine*, vol. lxv, pp. 690-692. Also *cf.* Giddings' system of social classification outlined in *An Introduction to the Study of Social Evolution*, by F. S. Chapin, pp. 209-231.

[3] Charlevoix, vol. iii, p. 260.

This scattered distribution of the early settlers was continually being complained of by the authorities,[1] as it left the colony an easy prey to the Indians;[2] but eventually it led to a more complete blending of the various elements in the population. This result was brought about by the fact that the authorities in their efforts to reduce the scattered distribution of the population did everything in their power to increase the rate of its growth. Especially did they endeavor to promote marriage.

It was usually single men,[3] in small groups of three or four, who pushed on to the frontier.[4] Later these single men were encouraged to marry either women from the older settlements,[5] or those brought over by private enterprise, or through the agency of the king.[6]

Talon's policy of disbanding soldiers in the colony and settling them on the land, still further helped to blend the population.[7] For, in order to strengthen the more vulner-

[1] Charlevoix, *op. cit.*, vol. iii, pp. 92-93, 309, 311; vol. iv, pp. 46, 264, 275.

[2] "As the French settlements are isolated, the Iroquois come in bands to kill the people and burn the homes when one least thinks of it." (*Rel.* 1675-1677, vol. lx, p. 135; *cf.* also *ibid.*, p. 143.

[3] Ferland, *op. cit.*, vol. i, p. 260.

[4] Charlevoix, *op. cit.*, vol. iii, p. 260.

[5] Sulte, *R. S. C., Trans.* 1905, sec. ii, p. 103.

[6] Very few of the early pioneers were in a position to do as is done by many of our immigrants to-day, who, after taking up land and becoming in better circumstances, return to their native provinces for wives. Not only was there the almost insurmountable difficulty of financing the voyage, but the state considered it "bad policy to allow colonists . . . to return to France." (*Canada and its Provinces*, vol. xv, *Quebec*, i, p. 52.)

[7] *Édits et Ord.* (1806), vol. ii, pp. 128e-128g. *Cf.* "In some parts of Canada are great tracts of land belonging to single persons; from these lands, pieces of forty arpents long and four wide are allowed to each discharged soldier who intends to settle here." (Kalm, *op. cit.*, vol. iii, p. 44.)

able and outlying communities, and to defend them more easily from Indian attacks, the soldiers who married and settled in the colony were distributed among these scattered communities,[1] or the seigniories of the officers.[2] In 1667 these soldier-settlers numbered 412 out of a total male population of 1,376 over 21 years of age.[3]

Thus, unlike many other early settlements in North America, the immigration to New France did not represent the transplanting of community groups of more or less closely related individuals. At its most flourishing period, 1667-1672,[4] it did not even represent an immigration of family groups, but as Parkman says, "it was mainly an immigration of single men and women." [5]

It is true, however, that previous to this, between 1632-1633, among the incoming settlers arriving from France there had been a considerable number of families. Occasionally small parties of three or four families more or less closely related were to be found among these immigrants.[6]

[1] And, secondly, the settling in the country both of officers—Captains, Lieutenants, and Ensigns, who unite themselves with the country by marriage, and secure fine grants, which they cultivate—and of the soldiers, who find good matches, and become scattered in all directions." (*Rel.* 1664-1667, vol. l, p. 245.)

[2] *Édits et Ord.* (1806), vol. ii, p. 128e *et seq.*

[3] *Census* 1667. The following passage from Kalm is also interesting: "This practice of disbanding soldiers in the colony seems to have been carried out more or less intermittently until the end of French rule." Kalm wrote in 1749 that, "One or two of the king's ships are annually sent from France to Canada, carrying recruits to supply the places of those soldiers who either died in the service or have got leave to settle in the country and turn farmers or to return to France. Almost every year they send a hundred or a hundred and fifty people over in this manner. With these people they likewise send over a great number of persons who have been found guilty of smuggling in France." (Kalm, vol. iii, p. 307.)

[4] Sulte, *R. S. C., Trans.* 1905, sec. ii, p. 114.

[5] Parkman, *Old Régime*, vol. ii, p. 26.

[6] Sulte, *op. cit.*, p. 111.

In 1634 the physician Giffard, brought "his whole household composed of many persons" to people his seigniory of Beauport.[1] Of the non-clerical population of 282, in 1640, 64 were married men and 64 married women. A considerable number of these must have been married before coming to New France; for, of the 106 boys and girls recorded, only 54 had been born in the colony.[2] Even after 1663, a fairly successful attempt was made by Talon, in 1669, to have families emigrate to the colony.[3] But on the whole, cases of families coming to New France were comparatively few. By far the greater number of settlers were unmarried men, who were compelled to seek their wives among the few girls already in the colony or among those who were being brought over from France. The fact that few family groups found their way into New France made the colony a virgin field for rapid and thorough amalgamation.

In order to overcome the inequality in the number of the sexes, so that the settlers might be provided with wives, large numbers of girls and women were brought over from France.[4] The Sulpicians at Montreal had been the first to aid female immigration to New France. The success of their efforts no doubt led the king to undertake and carry it on in a large way. These girls at first were drawn

[1] *Rel.* 1634-35, vol. vii, pp. 211, 213; *cf.* Ferland, *op. cit.*, vol. i, p. 266.

[2] Sulte, *op. cit.*, p. 111.

[3] Parkman, *Old Régime*, vol. ii, p. 26.

[4] "The king again sends us . . . sixty girls to populate the country." (*Rel.* 1664-1667, vol. l, p. 177; *cf.* also *ibid.*, pp. 215, 247; *Rel.* 1663-1665, vol. xliv, p. 161; *Rel.* 1666-1668, vol. li, p. 107.) "He has taken care to send over a few months ago a hundred and fifty girls, in order that the soldiers settling in New France may have families here." (*Rel.* 1669-1670, vol. liii, p. 37.) *Cf.* La Hontan (Pinkerton), *op. cit.*, p. 261; Charlevoix, *op. cit.*, vol. ii, p. 67.

largely from the homes for poor girls in the cities of Paris [1] and Lyons, one hundred coming during the summer of 1665.[2] Two years later eighty-four were sent from Dieppe and twenty-five from La Rochelle. These were apparently from a better class, since among them, it was said, were "fifteen or twenty of pretty good birth; several of them are really *demoiselles*, and tolerably well brought up." [3] As many of these city girls, however, did not make very good settlers' wives for a new country, efforts were directed to obtain girls, through the co-operation of the curés, from the rural districts.[4] In a letter of Colbert to the Archbishop of Rouen he suggested that, "in the parishes about Rouen, fifty or sixty girls might be found who would be glad to go to Canada to be married"; and he adds, "I beg you to employ your credit and authority with the curés of thirty or forty parishes to try to find in each of them one or two girls disposed to go voluntarily for the sake of a settlement in life." [5] These strong, healthy peasant girls were much sought after by the new settlers, because they could adapt themselves much more readily to the hardships of pioneer life. In 1672 only eleven girls had been sent out, because Talon had requested that, since the colonists had daughters just becoming of marriageable age, no more be sent from France for a time. Frontenac complained of this to Colbert, stating that "if a hundred and fifty girls and as many servants had been sent out this year, they

[1] "The ship from Normandy arrived, with 82 girls and women—among others, 50 from a charitable institution in Paris, where they have been well taught." (*Rel.* 1663-1665, vol. xlix, p. 169.)

[2] Parkman, *Old Régime*, vol. ii, p. 15.

[3] *Talon à Colbert*, 27 Oct., 1667, cited in Parkman, *ibid.*, pp. 15-16.

[4] Charlevoix, *op. cit.*, vol. iii, pp. 80-81.

[5] *Colbert à l'archevèque de Rouen*, 27 Feb., 1670, cited in Parkman, *Old Régime*, vol. ii, p. 18.

would all have received husbands and masters within a month." [1]

The method followed in bringing out girls from France further contributed to a thorough fusion of the various racial elements; both through the plan of recruiting the peasant girls from many different parishes throughout France,[2] and of arranging marriages on the arrival of the girls.[3]

In the arrangement of these marriages, as far as we know, no consideration was given to racial similarity. Selection was determined largely on the economic rating of the prospective husbands, and the attractiveness, physical and otherwise, of the girls. To facilitate this plan, the girls were divided into three different groups, and La Hontan says, "the sparks that wanted to be married made their addresses to the . . . governesses, to whom they were obliged to give an account of their goods and estates before they were allowed to make their choice in the three seraglios." [4]

Until the British conquest in 1759, marriage in New France was free from the impediments of racial or religious differences. The charter establishing the Company of One Hundred Associates had specifically ordered that only French Catholics should be permitted to live in the colony.[5] From time to time, notwithstanding, some Huguenots found their way into the colony. Few, however, were allowed to remain unless they abjured their faith.[6] In the commission

[1] *Frontenac à Colbert*, 2 Nov., 1672, cited in Parkman, *Old Régime*, vol. ii, p. 16.

[2] *Colbert à l'archevèque de Rouen, 27 Fév., 1670*, cited in *ibid.*, p. 18.

[3] *Talon à Colbert*, 10 Nov., 1670, cited in *ibid.*, p. 19.

[4] La Hontan (Pinkerton), p. 261. [5] *Édits et Ord.* (1803), vol. i, p. 3.

[6] "A number of Heretics being among these troops, efforts were exerted, and successfully, for their conversion; more than a score made abjuration of their heresy." (*Rel.* 1664-1667, vol. l, p. 85; *cf. Jugements et Délib.*, vol. i, pp. 262-263; Salone, *op. cit.*, p. 45; *C. A.*, B. 74, pt. i, p. 50.)

of the king to the governor and *Intendant*, in 1665, instructions had been very explicit. They were to use their influence, "to bring the people to a knowledge of God and the light of the faith and of the Catholic religion, apostolic and Roman, and to establish the exercise of it to the exclusion of all other."[1] Every ship seems to have been watched for heretics,[2] and such severe pressure was brought to bear on all classes alike, that nothing was left for the Protestant intending to make a home in New France, but to recant.[3] Many conversions are recorded, especially among those who through illness found their way to the hospitals.[4] Consequently, the number of Protestants in the colony, during the French régime, was always so small as to constitute practically no impediment to amalgamation.

Every encouragement was given to marriage, and especially to early marriage. Boys and girls who married under twenty and sixteen years respectively, received from the crown twenty *livres* each.[5] To girls sent out from France by the king's order a dowry, called "the present of the king," was given on their marriage.[6] Even more was done to encourage marriage among the *noblesse*. La Motte, of

[1] *Édits et Ord.* (1806), vol. ii, p. 36.

[2] *Rel.* 1664-1667, vol. l, p. 85.

[3] A captain of one of Monseigneur de Tracy's companies made his abjuration of heresy in the principal church. (*Rel.* 1663-65, vol. xlix, p. 169.)

[4] "Among the patients coming to our hospital there were many diseased both in body and in soul. Some were Huguenots; and, thanks be to God, they all made public abjuration of their heresy.' (*Rel.* 1663-1665, vol. xlix, p. 203; *cf. ibid.*, p. 169; *Rel.* 1656-57, vol. xliii, pp. 33-35; *Rel.* 1659-60, vol. xlv, p. 71; *Rel.* 1664-67, vol. l, pp. 85, 87, 155; *Rel.* 1666-68, vol. li, p. 109.)

[5] *Édits et Ord.* (1803), vol. i, p. 58.

[6] *Ibid.*, vol. i, p. 58; *cf.* also La Hontan (Pinkerton), *op. cit.*, p. 262; Parkman, *Old Régime*, vol. ii, p. 21.

the Carignan-Salières regiment, was given 1500 *livres* for marrying and settling in the country. A further sum of 6000 *livres* was given to the other officers who married, and a fund of 12,000 *livres* was set aside to provide encouragement for others who would follow their example.[1] The court considered it of the utmost concern that all should be married. Colbert urged Talon,

> to commend it to the consideration of the whole people, that their prosperity, their substance, and all that is dear to them depend upon a general resolution never to be departed from, to marry youths of eighteen or nineteen years and girls at fourteen or fifteen; since abundance can never come to them except through an abundance of men.[2]

On the other hand, severe pressure was brought to bear upon those who delayed marriage. Parents, whose boys of twenty years and girls of sixteen remained unmarried, were to be subject to a fine.[3] Before the ships arrived from France with girls, Talon issued orders that all single men were expected to be married within a fortnight after the arrival of the ships.[4] Unmarried men were even forbidden by Talon the right to fish, hunt, trade with the Indians, or to go into the woods.[5] Obdurate bachelors, Colbert wrote, "should be made to bear additional burdens, and be excluded from all honors; it would be well even to add some marks of infamy."[6] It was not likely that the unmarried officers were subject to any such constraint. La Hontan, however, makes it clear that social and even ecclesiastical

[1] *Colbert à Talon, 20 Fév., 1668*, cited in Parkman, *ibid.*, pp. 14-15.

[2] *Ibid.*

[3] *Édits et Ord.* (1803), vol. i, p. 58.

[4] Parkman, *Old Régime*, vol. ii, p. 22.

[5] *Talon au Ministre*, 10 Oct., 1670; *ibid.*, p. 22.

[6] *Lettre du 20 Fév., 1668*, cited in *ibid.*, p. 23.

pressure was not wanting to induce the officers to marry, remarking that "after a man has made four visits to a young woman, he is obliged to unfold his mind to her father and mother; he must either talk of marriage, or if he does not, both he and she lie under a scandal," and that he knew of "several young women, whose lovers after denying the fact, and proving before the judges the scandalous conversations of their mistresses, were forced, upon the persuasion of the ecclesiastics, to swallow the bitter pill, and take the same girls in marriage." "In fine," he says, "most of the officers marry in this country." [1]

These efforts to encourage marriage met with a large measure of success, as is seen by the following census returns. Among the total population of 3,315 in 1665-1666, there were 1061 or 32 per cent either married or widowed; in 1667, with a population of 3918, there were 1296 or 33.07 per cent either married or widowed; in 1685, with a population of 12,263, there were 4218 or 34.4 per cent either married or widowed; and in 1688, with a population of 11,562, there were 4288 or 37.17 per cent either married or widowed.[2] This shows an increase in the proportion of married persons to the total population of 5.17 per cent, during the period of greatest stimulation.[3]

The statistics of age in relation to marriage show that, in 1665-1666, of the 491 married women, 8 or 1.63 per cent were between the ages of 11 and 15 years, which was 8 per cent of all the girls between those ages; that 45 or 9.16 per cent were between the ages of 16 and 20 years, which was 69.23 per cent of all the girls between these ages; and that 239 or 46.64 per cent were between the ages

1 La Hontan (Pinkerton), *op. cit.*, pp. 366-367.

2 *Censuses* 1665-1666, 1667, 1685, 1688.

3 Owing to the rapid increase of the population under marriageable age these different periods are not strictly comparable.

of 21 or 30 years, which was 91.57 per cent of all the women between these ages. Of the 167 women between the ages of 31 and 50 years only 3.6 per cent were unmarried. Among the male population of 1250 at 21 years and over, only 528 or 42.25 per cent were married, 120 or 9.9 per cent of these were between 21 and 30 years of age, and none were under 21 years.

According to the census of 1667 there were 626 married women. Of these only 2, or .032 per cent, were between the ages of 11 and 15 years, which was 1.7 per cent of all the girls in this age-group, a considerably smaller percentage than in the previous census. The number of married between the ages of 16 and 21, however, was larger than in the previous census, being 65 or 13.8 per cent, which was 63.72 per cent of all the girls between the ages of 16 and 20 years; while 267, or 41.5 per cent, were between the ages of 21 and 30 years, which was 92.39 per cent of all the women between 21 and 30. Of the 246 women between the ages of 31 and 50 years, 21, or 6.5 per cent, were unmarried. This increase over the previous enumeration would seem to indicate that not all of the women sent out from France were under 30 years of age. The proportion of married men of 21 years and over to the total number is slightly smaller, being only 40 per cent as compared with 42.25 per cent. One boy, however, between 16 and 20 was reported as married.[1] Marriages are on record of girls as young as 12 and 13 years of age.[2]

Not only was encouragement given to marriage, but inducements were held out for large families. The king's edict of April, 1670 declared,

in order to increase the number of children . . . that in future all inhabitants of Canada who shall have children living to

[1] *Censuses* 1665-1666 and 1667.

[2] *Rel.* 1650-1651, vol. xxxvi, p. 246 *cf. Rel.* 1656-1657, vol. xliii, p. 321.

the number of ten, born in legitimate wedlock, not being priests, monks, or nuns, shall be paid out of the moneys sent by his majesty to said country a pension of 300 *livres* a year, and those who shall have twelve, 400 *livres;* and that to this effect they shall be required to present to the *Intendant* of justice, police and finance, established in the said country, the number of their children in the month of June or July of each year; who, having verified the same, shall order the payment of the said pensions, half in cash and the other half at the end of each year.[1]

Furthermore, those having the largest families in their respective parishes and communities were to have the preference, both as regards rank in the church, and position of honor in the local community. The edict required:

That there be made by the Sovereign Council situated at Quebec for the said province, a general division of all the inhabitants by parishes and villages and that there be given some honors to the principal inhabitants who will take part in the affairs of each village or community, either according to their rank in the church or otherwise; and that those inhabitants who have the greater number of children be always preferred to the others, unless some good reasons prevent it.[2]

These measures of the king, under the progressive policy of Colbert, had a marked influence in stimulating the birth-rate during this period,[3] and in establishing a fecundity among the French Canadians exceeded only in recent years by Roumania.[4] Bishop Laval, in a letter in 1668,

[1] *Edits et Ord.* (1803), vol. i, pp. 57-58.

[2] *Ibid.*

[3] "The people multiply here at least twice as fast as in France." *Rel.* 1664-1667, vol. 1, p. 179.

[4] During the period 1903-1911 the minimum birth-rate in Quebec was 358 and the maximum 412 per 10,000. *Quebec Statistical Year Book,* 1914, p. 91.

wrote, "in this country there are generally 8, 10, 12, and sometimes as many as 15 and 16 children."[1] According to the census returns for 1665-1666, the percentage of the population under one year was 5.38; for 1667, 5.82; and for 1681, 4.64.[2] These percentages are more than equivalent[3] to a birth-rate of 538, 582, and 464 per 10,000 for these years.

Furthermore, the social barriers which prevented marriage between the different classes finally gave way with the decline of the seigniorial system, and the widening of economic and educational advantages. The *noblesse* represented the landed aristocracy in New France, and were drawn from the nobility in France, and the military and civil officials who settled in the colony.[4]

In the early period of the colony the *noblesse* had been able to maintain their station with considerable dignity and exclusiveness; and "as far as their means permitted in the Château of St. Louis they imitated the splendour and ceremony of the court of Versailles."[5] While never a very numerous class, yet as seigniors, and military and civil officials, they had considerable influence with the *bourgeoisie*

[1] *Rel.* 1667-1669, vol. lii, p. 49.

[2] *Censuses* 1665-1666, 1667 and 1681.

[3] The number of children born in any year preceding any census date is equivalent to the number of living children under one year enumerated in the census plus the number of children under one year who died during the preceding year. The infant mortality in Quebec then was in all probability even higher before 1681 than it is now. Talon reported in 1671 that between 600 and 700 children had been born in the colony during the year (*Talon à Colbert,* 2 Nov., 1671), while the actual returns for 1681, with at least twice the population, gave the total number of children under one year as only 449. (*Census,* 1681.)

[4] *Const. Docs.*, vol. i, p. 59.

[5] *A Political and Historical Account of Lower Canada,* ascribed to either De Salles or Latterrière, p. 115.

and *habitants.*[1] After the British conquest many returned to France.[2] Masères states that in 1774 there were twenty-two families of *noblesse* in Canada;[3] and Governor Carleton, in his testimony in the House of Commons, in the same year, estimated their numbers at 150.[4]

Many of the *noblesse*, during the latter period of French rule, had found it economically impossible to maintain the former social status of their families, and some had gradually sunk to the level of the *habitant.*[5] After the conquest, however, the situation of those who remained was rendered still more difficult. About seventy of these had been in the French service in the colony;[6] and as the British government did not even recognize their rank,[7] much less make any official provision for them, they found it increasingly difficult to maintain their station.[8]

But the greatest cause of the decline of the nobility was their aversion to work, and their desire to live as "*gentils-hommes de compagne*" as in France.[9] Second only to their dislike for farm work, was their disgust for trade,[10] and

[1] *C. A.*, Q., vol. 5, pt. i, p. 262.

[2] Francis Masères, *Proceedings of the British . . . to obtain an House of Assembly . . .*, p. 165.

[3] *Ibid.*

[4] Sir Henry Cavendish, *Debates of the House of Commons in the Year 1774*, p. 107.

[5] "He represents that there are many families of Gentlemen, very worthy persons in extreme want, not even having bread, and solicits some charity for them." (Denonville to the Minister, *Colon. Docs. N. Y.*, vol. ix, p. 317; *cf.* Duchesneau to the Minister, Nov. 10, 1679, cited by Munro, *Docs. S. T.*, pp. 49-53.)

[6] *C. A.*, Q. 5, pt. i, p. 263.

[7] Cavendish, *op. cit.*, pp. 118, 119.

[8] *C. A.*, Q. 5, pt. i, p. 263.

[9] Duchesneau to the Minister, Nov. 10, 1679; cited by Munro, *op. cit.*, p. 49.

[10] "The Genteel people of the country despise merchants." *C. A.*, Q. 2, p. 378; *cf.* also Milnes to Portland, cited by Egerton and Grant, *Select Speeches and Dispatches Relating to the Constitutional History of Canada*, p. 111.

their contempt for the educational opportunities offered in the colony for their children. Over against these factors, which were undermining their social and economic status, was the growth, after the conquest, of democratic ideals, and the widening of opportunities for economic independence afforded the trading and merchant classes. The *noblesse*, now no longer able to maintain their isolation by privilege, or superior wealth or intelligence, ceased to exist as a separate class.[1] Heterogeneity in social classes ceased to be of importance.

[1] "The English introduced among the population a spirit of traffic; they taught them to appreciate the advantages of individual wealth and to feel that a man might be of importance even though not descended from a noble race. . . . The *bourgeoisie* . . . of the towns caught the spirit—laboured, and laboured successfully, to accumulate wealth for themselves; and being a frugal and prudent race, they quickly found themselves possessed of fortunes more than sufficient to cope with the broken-down *noblesse* around them. They, therefore, immediately began to compete with this fading generation both in political and social life. The nobles . . . looked with disdain upon the occupation of a merchant. To obtain their own livelihood they considered a degradation. To live upon the labour of others they deemed honorable prerogative. In the present state of affairs, however, they possessed no power to wring from other men the means of splendour or subsistence; being idle, they became wretchedly poor. The old *noblesse*, unfortunate for themselves, neglected the education of their children; France was no longer before them as a model to be imitated or a seminary for instruction. . . . To the Canadian seminaries of instruction they paid little attention, supposing them incapable of conveying that species of knowledge which they desired. . . . The children of these noble families were consequently brought up in idleness and ignorance. The *bourgeoisie*, in the mean time, having themselves acquired riches, sought out for means of imparting instruction to their children. Their own seminaries were alone within their power; and not being diverted by higher aspirations, they contented themselves with improving that which they possessed. The rising generation received a fair and useful education, by the aid of the priesthood; and were thus enabled to surpass their noble competitors in knowledge as their fathers had before surpassed them in wealth. . . . When the people thought it of importance to have efficient members in the House of Representatives,

To summarize the points of this chapter, it has been shown that the outcome of the demographic conditions in Canada before 1791 was the development of a highly homogeneous population. The magnificent system of waterways, on the one hand, provided an easy means of access to the newer districts while the seigniorial system of land tenure on the other, tended to multiply scattered communities. Within the local settlements, however, the relatively dense populations along the river banks and the unusual opportunities for inter-communication among the inhabitants gradually developed a high degree of mental unity.

The conditions of life were hard, but for the industrious and persevering there was a plentiful food supply which made possible a rapid increase in population. Immigration drawn from all parts of France, coupled with the widespread distribution of the immigrants on their arrival in the colony, prepared the way for the thorough amalgamation of the early French stock, so that the encouragement given by the government to early marriage and large families soon made the French Canadian population a much more homogeneous aggregation than even the population of France.

the men of action and education, viz. the *bourgeoisie*, were immediately selected and the nobles passed from the stage at once and forever." (*A Pol. and Hist. Account of L. C.*, pp. 115-117.)

CHAPTER III

Social and Moral Solidarity

The homogeneity of race in the population of New France emphasized in the preceding chapter, is not more striking than the very definite type of social and moral solidarity which resulted from it. In trying to discover the chief features of this unity, one cannot fail to be struck with the remarkable degree of homogeneity existing in occupation, language, religion and social customs, and to note the absence of differentiating interests both within and without the church. These conditions, as well as the type of mind and character that was developed among the French Canadians, have constituted the chief factors in the remarkable social and moral solidarity which was developed.

The uniformity in occupation is strikingly brought out by the fact that after the restoration of Canada to the French in 1632, agriculture, from a small beginning, steadily gained in importance until it became the leading industry of New France. The fur trade, although receiving the chief attention of the trading companies, does not appear to have been considered of first importance, after 1640, by the people themselves. Even after 1674, when the monopoly of the fur companies had been withdrawn,[1] and private fur trading was at its height, probably at least sixty per cent of the population were still engaged in agriculture.

The census of 1681 showed that 372 males, or only 11.6 per cent of all the men between the ages of 21 and 70 years,[2]

[1] *Edits et Ord.* (1803), vol. i, pp. 63-67.

[2] *Census*, 1681.

were engaged in the trades, commerce, and the professions. Eight hundred, or 24.9 per cent, according to the estimate of the *Intendant* Duchesneau, in 1680,[1] were trappers or *voyageurs*, or what were more commonly called *coureurs de bois.*[2] The remaining 2037, or 63 per cent, must have been engaged in agricultural pursuits.[3] In 1695, 9769 of the total population of 12,786, or 76.4 per cent, were living in the rural parishes.[4] In 1739, 33,510 of the total popu-

[1] Duchesneau's estimate of 800 *coureurs de bois* was probably in excess of the actual number, if we may judge by his estimate of the total population at 10,679, which was shown, by actual enumeration the following year, to have been only 9,677. (*Census*, 1681.) Duchesneau, in another estimate, places the number of the *coureurs de bois* at 500: "What I have written on the subject of the number and long absence of the *coureurs de bois*, my Lord, justifies sufficiently my representation that this country was diminishing in population and that the farms were uncultivated. Two years' absence of five hundred persons (according to the lowest calculation), the best adapted to farm work, cannot increase agriculture; and this is confirmed by the complaints of seigniors, who do not participate in the profits of the *coureurs de bois*, that they cannot find men to do their work." (M. Duchesneau to M. de Seignelay, *Colon. Docs. N. Y.*, vol. ix, p. 151.) Evidently the estimate of 800 was sufficiently large to include all those engaged in the fur trade. The licensed fur-traders could never have been many, for the edict only provided that licenses should be granted for 25 canoes, with three men to each canoe, or 75 men in all. "His Majesty was graciously pleased to grant an amnesty to the disobedient, with authority to issue twenty-five licenses yearly to twenty-five canoes, having each three men, to trade among the savages; and in order that the favor might not be abused, his Majesty, by his edict, enacted punishments against those who should go trading without license." (Memoir of M. Duchesneau on Irregular Trade in Canada, *Colon. Docs. N. Y.*, vol. ix, p. 159.) This edict was revoked and restored a number of times, and restored finally in 1726, but the number of licenses or the number of men to a canoe was never increased. (*Ibid.*, pp. 159, 954, 958; *cf.* also *Rel.* 1696-1702, vol. lxv, p. 272; *Edits et Ord.* (1803), vol. i, pp. 258, 330; La Hontan, pp. 329, 330, 333 and 283; Charlevoix, vol. iii, pp. 195, 310; vol. iv, p. 275.)

[2] *Cf.* citation to *Coureurs de bois*, pp. 60-61.

[3] *Census*, 1681.

[4] *Census*, 1695.

lation of 42,701, or 71.5 per cent, were living in the rural parishes;[1] and in 1754, 42,200 of the total population of 55,009, or 76.7 per cent, were living in the rural parishes.[2]

After the conquest, with the decline of the fur trade, and the passing of general trading more and more into the hands of the British, the proportion of French Canadians in the rural parishes steadily increased. In 1765, 54,466 of the total population of 69,810,[3] or 78 per cent, were in the rural parishes; and in 1790, 128,098 of the total population of 161,311,[4] or 79.4 per cent, were to be found in the rural parishes. With the English population growing more rapidly in the cities and towns, it is most probable that at the end of our period (1791), over 80 per cent of French Canadians were living in the open country, or in small rural villages, and possessing all the traditionalism and conservatism, peculiar to a homogeneous agricultural population.

Uniformity of language further intensified the social solidarity resulting from uniformity of occupation. At the time of the conquest French was practically the only language spoken. Although immigrants had been drawn from all parts of New France, and many from provinces where little, if any, French was spoken, so complete had been the fusion of these early settlers, among whom the French-speaking predominated, that, in a comparatively short time, the French language had received universal acceptance.

[1] *Census*, 1739.

[2] *Census*, 1754.

[3] This includes an estimated population for Quebec and Montreal of 14,700, and also that of Three Rivers by actual enumeration of 644. (*Census*, 1765.)

[4] This includes an estimated population for Quebec and Montreal of 32,000 and also the population of Three Rivers, by enumeration, of 1,213. (*Census*, 1790.)

After the conquest, there was a desire on the part of the British gradually to introduce English. The opposition, however, which the government had met with in attempting to introduce English law had, to some extent, called its attention to the seriousness of the language problem. This opposition was soon to take organized form. During the readings of the Quebec Act, the representative of the French Canadians urged upon the British Parliament that not only should no attempt be made to introduce the English language, and that all officials sent out from England should be familiar with French, but also that French should be the official language.[1] The chief request of the petition was not granted, although it most probably influenced Parliament, in making French equal with English as the official language of Quebec.[2]

[1] "And lastly, one point which deserves attention and which ought to be settled, is that the French language being the general, and indeed almost the only language used in Canada, it is obvious that no stranger who goes there, having only his own interests at heart, can serve them well, except as he is thoroughly versed in this language, and obliged to make use of it continually in all the special matters which he has on hand; that it is completely impossible, taking into account the distance between the establishments and the dwellings throughout the country, ever to attempt to introduce the English language generally; for all these reasons, and others not here specified, it is indispensable that the French language should be ordered to be the only one employed in everything which deals with and shall be settled as a public business, whether in the courts of justice or in the assembly of the legislative corps, &c., for it would be a cruel thing to attempt to reduce unnecessarily almost all those interested in public affairs to the condition of never being acquainted henceforth with what shall be discussed or decided throughout the country." (Chartier de Lotbiniere, *Const. Docs.*, vol. i, p. 399.)

[2] "That bills relative to the criminal laws of England in force in this province, and to the rights of the Protestant Clergy, as specified in the act of the 31st year of his Majesty, Chap. 31, shall be introduced in the English language; and the Bills relative to the Laws, customs, usages and civil rights of this Province, shall be introduced in the French language, in order to preserve the unity of the texts. That such bills

This attained, the hierarchy was not slow to recognize in the French language the strongest bulwark of Catholicism against the Anglicizing influences of their conquerors. Their ability to retain control of education furnished the means of perpetuating the French language; with the result that every effort of the government and the Church of England to establish public schools for the teaching of English in the parishes,[1] was frustrated by the opposition of the hierarchy. The *bourgeois*, it was true, soon became more or less familiar with English,[2] but the great mass of the people knew only one language.[3]

In this way the French language, in the hands of the church, became an effective weapon of isolation, warding off modernism in every form. For, on the one hand, English

as are presented shall be put into both languages; that those in English be put into French, and those presented in French be put into English by the Clerk of the House or his assistants, according to the directions they may receive, before they be read the first time—and when so put shall also be read each time in both languages—well understood that each member has a right to bring in any bill in his own language, but that after the same shall be translated, the text shall be considered to be that of the language of the law to which said bill hath reference." (Extracts from the Rules and Regulations of the House of Assembly, Lower Canada, *Const. Docs.*, vol. ii, p. 105.)

[1] *C. A.*, Q. 86, pt. 2, p. 372; *cf.* also *ibid.*, Q. 48, pt. ii, p. 673; Q. 86, pt. i, p. 96; Q. 84, p. 293; Q. 84, p. 273.

[2] *Pol. and Hist. Account of L. C.*, p. 163.

[3] ". . . and more especially it is notorious that they have not hitherto made any progress toward the attainment of the language of the country under whose government they have the happiness to live. This total ignorance of the English language on the part of the Canadians draws a distinct line of demarcation between them and His Majesty's British subjects in this province, alike injurious to the welfare and happiness of both; and continues to divide into two separate peoples those who by their situation, their common interests and their equal participation of the same laws and the same form of Government should naturally form one people. . . ." (Bishop [Ang.] to Lieut. Gov. Milnes, *C. A.*, Q. 84, p. 188; *cf.* also *ibid.*, p. 273.)

ideas were successfully shut out, and on the other, all French literature was so carefully censored that only those French ideas which were in complete harmony with the church were allowed to get in.[1] The barrier of language thus became another stepping stone in the rise of ecclesiastical control. Uniformity of language, however, was not the only factor which, by intensifying social solidarity, made ecclesiastical control easy.

The absence of interests and organizations other than the church contributed powerfully to this result by confining the leadership of the social life of the people to the church alone. The whole system of both church and state tended to curb initiative. The church demanded an unquestioned obedience. "Humility, obedience, purity, meekness, modesty, simplicity, chastity and charity"[2] were the chief virtues: independence of judgment, and the quest for truth had no place. "Humility and obedience head the list; for in unquestioning submission to the spiritual director lay the guaranty of all other merits."[3] So severe and offensive did La Mothe-Cadillac consider the authority assumed by the clergy that he says, "Neither men of honor nor men of parts are endured in Canada; nobody can live here but simpletons and slaves of the ecclesiastical domination."[4]

[1] "They prohibit and burn all the books that treat of any other subject but devotion. When I think of this tyranny I cannot but be enraged at the impertinent zeal of the curate of this city. This inhuman fellow came one day to my lodging, and finding the romance of the *Adventures of Petronius* upon my table, he fell upon it with an unimaginable fury, and tore out almost all the leaves." (La Hontan Pinkerton ed., *op. cit.*, p. 279; *cf.* also *C. A.*, M. 384, p. 106.)

[2] *Ancien réglement du Petit Séminaire de Québec,* cited by Parkman, *Old Régime*, vol. ii, p. 163.

[3] Parkman, *Old Régime*, vol. ii, p. 163; *cf.* pp. 145-155.

[4] *La Mothe-Cadillac à 28 Sept., 1694,* cited by Parkman, vol. viii, p. 151; *cf.* La Hontan, p. 297.

The state discouraged its citizens from having any voice in directing public affairs. They were not even permitted to associate with one another for the regulation of their local municipal affairs. The land tenure, while it promoted the *habitant's* immediate comfort, was singularly successful in checking his desire to better his condition. The whole influence was unimproving and repressive, and practically rendered impossible the development of an active and progressive people.[1]

The repressive policy of both church and state was, moreover, rendered less difficult among the settled population by the tendency of the young men to become *coureurs de bois*.[2] These restless spirits, who were unable to withstand the repression and restraint of the parishes, sought the freedom of the interior. Denonville writes:

This has come to pass, that, from the moment a boy can carry a gun, the father cannot restrain him and dares not offend him. You can judge the mischief that followed. These disorders are always greatest in the families of those who are *gentilshommes*, or who through laziness or vanity pass themselves off as such. Having no resource but hunting, they

[1] Durham, p. 16; *cf*. Cahall, *The Sovereign Council of New France*, p. 22; *Can. and its Prov.*, vol. xv, Quebec, i, pp. 287-288.

[2] "Against absolute authority there was a counter influence, rudely and wildly antagonistic. Canada was at the very portal of the great interior wilderness. The St. Lawrence and the Lakes were the highway to the domain of savage freedom; and thither the disenfranchised, half-starved seignior, and the discouraged *habitant* who could find no market for his produce, naturally enough betook themselves. Their lessons of savagery were well learned, and for many a year a boundless license and stiff-handed authority battled for the control of Canada. Nor to the last were Church and state fairly masters of the field. French rule was drawing towards its close when the intendant complained that though twenty-eight companies of regular troops were quartered in the colony, there were not soldiers enough to keep the people in order." (Parkman, *Old Régime*, vol. ii, p. 198.)

must spend their lives in the woods, where they have no curés to trouble them and no fathers or guardians to constrain them . . . I cannot tell you, *monseigneur*, how attractive this Indian life is to all our youth. It consists in doing nothing, caring nothing, following every inclination, and getting out of the way of all correction.[1]

The removal of this young, restless, and radical element in the population, while a direct loss economically and socially to the settled communities and to the Indian settlements of the Upper country,[2] nevertheless, left in the home parish a more fertile soil for the abnormal growth of the absolute authority of church and state. These same men as *coureurs de bois* often gave themselves over to lewdness and carousing and thus became a double loss to the colony.

The pressure of pioneer life, in a heavily timbered country where money and farm labor were scarce,[3] left little time for leisure. The men who resisted the lure of the fur trade and remained on the land were "habituated to the incessant labor of a rude and unskilled agriculture,"[4] where many fields had still to be hewn out of the forest. The women, too, because of early marriage and proverbially large fami-

[1] Cited by Parkman, *Old Régime*, vol. ii, pp. 177-178; *cf.* Charlevoix, vol. v, p. 286.

[2] "For it is evident that the latter method serves but to depopulate the country of all its young men; to reduce the number of people in the houses; to deprive wives of their husbands, fathers and mothers of the aid of their children, and sisters of that of their brothers; to expose those who undertake such journeys to a thousand dangers for both their bodies and their souls . . . which, if viewed in the proper light, caused more loss than profit to the country, because, at the same time when it acquires some beaver skins for the Colony, it deprives it forever of the labor of all the young men, by accustoming them to be unable and unwilling to do any more work." (*Rel.* 1696-1702, vol. lxv, pp. 219-221.)

[3] *Colon. Docs. N. Y.*, vol. ix, pp. 151, 398.

[4] Durham, p. 16.

lies, as well as their activities both in the house and out, had little time for anything except the more elemental things of life.[1]

Under these conditions, there was little opportunity for developing new interests among the *habitants*. The absence of other interests undoubtedly had a large part in giving the church such a large place in the life of the French Canadians. Of community organizations there were none. Political associations, secret societies and labor unions had no place in the life of the French Canadian. The St. Jean-Baptiste society, which in recent years under the guise of religion has become such a strong political organization, did not exist. Thus during our period, the church was completely free from competing organizations, unless the militia may be so classed.[2] The public and high schools which to-day, in many agricultural districts, share the community leadership, were in Quebec mere agencies of the church.[3]

The social solidarity already attributed in large part to

[1] "In their knowledge of economy they greatly surpass the English women in the plantations, who indeed have taken the liberty of throwing all the burthen of housekeeping upon their husbands, and sit in their chairs all day with folded arms. The women in Canada, on the contrary, do not spare themselves, especially among the common people, where they are always in the fields, meadows, stables, &c., and do not dislike any work whatsoever. . . . And I have with pleasure seen the daughters of the better sort of people, and of the governor himself, not too finely dressed, and going into the kitchen and cellars, to look that everything be done as it ought." (Kalm, *Travels in North America*, vol. iii, pp. 56-57.)

[2] "The Canadians are formed into a militia, for the better regulation of which, each parish in proportion to its extent and number of inhabitants, is divided into one, two, or more companies, who have their proper officers, captains, lieutenants, ensigns, majors, aide-majors, sergeants, &c., and all orders or public regulations are addressed to the captains or commanding officers, who are to see the same put into execution." (Report of General Murray, *Const. Docs.*, vol. i, p. 41.)

[3] *Infra*, pp. 82-94.

the homogeneity of population which resulted from situation and various artificial features, was further due to the fact that the sources of subsistence were relatively uniform. Little diversity of occupation was possible. The vast majority of the people were thus subjected to relatively simple and uniform stimuli in the process of exploiting their environment and gaining a living. Continued like-response to such common stimuli, is of course the most important, if not the only means of developing social solidarity.[1] In this process of repeated common stimulation the parish church was the centre, social, political and religious. The social intercourse and enjoyment centering around the church on Sunday, as well as on the numerous church holidays, was a strong feature in the life of the community.[2] Community leadership also very largely was to be found in the church. The priest's voice had the strongest note of authority then as now in the community. In fact the parish church was the embodiment of community solidarity.[3]

The characteristics of the French Canadians during our

[1] Franklin H. Giddings, *Inductive Sociology*, pp. 57, 60-68; *Historical and Descriptive Sociology*, pp. 124-125, 128 *et seq.*, 311-312.

[2] "In Canada . . . many of the people's enjoyments are connected with their religious ceremonies; the Sunday is to them their day of gaiety; there is then an assemblage of friends and relatives; the parish church collects together all whom they know, with whom they have relations of business and pleasure; the young and old, men and women, clad in their best garments, riding their best horses, driving in their best *calèches,* meet there for purposes of business, love and pleasure. . . . In short, Sunday is the grand fête, it forms the most pleasurable part of the *habitant's* life; rob them of their Sunday, you rob them of what, in their eyes, renders life most worthy of possession." (*A Pol. and Hist. Account of L. C.*, pp. 120-121.)

[3] "It has been rightly observed that the religious observances of the French Canadians are so intermingled with all their business and all their amusements that the priest and the church are with them, more than with any other people, the centres of their little communities." (Durham, *op. cit.*, p. 98.)

period also made them readily subject to ecclesiastical control. The prevailing type of character was forceful and convivial.[1] The first of these qualities is seen in the eagerness with which the *habitants* advanced further and further out on the frontier, willingly facing the dangers incident to pioneer life in a new country,[2] in the zest with which the young men sought the free, reckless life of the *coureurs de bois*, penetrating far into the interior,[3] and in their hardihood and daring in battle such that it was said of them that they "are brave, well disciplined and indefatigable on the march."[4] M. de Vaudreuil in his letter to M. de Massiac wrote, in regard to the Canadians then fighting in the king's troops,

They have rendered the greatest services;—they clearly perceive the importance made of them each time they are wanted. They bear without a murmur the *corvées* with which they are continually burthened. They ask nothing better than to be placed in the most exposed situations, either in encampment scouting parties, and even in front of the enemy. They distinguished themselves on the day of the 8th.[5]

Their conviviality is shown in a love for social intercourse and amusement. Driving and visiting, attending parties and dances, smoking and public drinking, were among the more popular diversions, especially during the long winter season. Charlevoix writes,

Everybody does his part to make the time pass pleasantly, with

[1] Giddings, *Inductive Sociology*, pp. 82-83; *Historical and Descriptive Sociology*, pp. 214-229, 233-236.

[2] *Cf. supra*, pp. 17-18.

[3] *Cf. supra*, p. 55.

[4] *Colon. Docs. N. Y.*, vol. ix, p. 725.

[5] *Ibid.*, vol. x, p. 780; *cf. ibid.*, pp. 1000-1001, 1039, 1076, 1083. This statement of Vaudreuil's is at least open to question, for Montcalm complained that the French Canadian militia "know neither discipline or subordination" (Parkman, *Montcalm and Wolfe*, vol. ii, p. 152; *cf.* pp. 148-158).

games and parties of pleasure,—drives and canoe excursions in summer, sleighing and skating in winter. There is a great deal of hunting and shooting for many Canadian gentlemen are almost destitute of any other means of living at their ease.[1]

Another keen observer in describing the amusements of the people about a century later writes as follows,

The chief pleasures of the inhabitants consist at this time [winter] in carioling and visiting each other. Churchgoing, visiting, purchasing, in short every journey, whether of pleasure or business is performed in the cariole. . . . Not only is there a cessation from the labor but a constant round of parties and dancing of which the whole people are passionately fond. . . . The people assemble not merely to see one another, but with a serious intention of enjoying themselves . . . they dance with spirit and eat with vigor. . . . At their weddings the same custom prevails; a dance and a feasting always succeed this happy event.[2]

Smoking and drinking were very common. Kalm says, with regard to smoking and the use of snuff,

Every farmer plants a quantity of tobacco near his house, in proportion to the size of his family. It is likewise very necessary that they should plant tobacco, because it is universally smoked by the common people. Boys often of twelve years of age, run about with the pipe in their mouths, as well as the old people. . . . People of both sexes, and of all ranks, use snuff very much.[3]

The drink habit from a very early period wrought havoc

[1] Charlevoix, cited by Parkman, *Old Régime*, vol. ii, p. 195; *cf. Memoires sur le Canada*, p. 208.

[2] *A Pol. and Hist. Account of L. C.*, pp. 133-134.

[3] Kalm, *op. cit.*, vol. viii, pp. 253-254.

not only among the Indians but the colonists as well.[1] Denonville and Champigny, in a letter to the Minister on the evils of the brandy traffic point out that

> The Canadians also ruin their health thereby, and as the greater number of them drink a large quantity of it [brandy] early in the morning, they are incapable of doing anything the remainder of the day . . . so that it is considered absolutely necessary to find means to diminish its use among the Canadians. . . .[2]

A contemporary well described this prevalent type of character: " The Canadians are . . . robust, vigorous, and accustomed in time of need to live on little. They have intelligence and vivacity, but are wayward, light-minded, and inclined to debauchery ".[3]

Their apparent light-hearted indifference to the future, coupled with a love of ostentation and display, occasioned much extravagance among the people, especially the *noblesse* and *bourgeoisie,* which often brought them to the verge of bankruptcy. Charlevoix contrasts this trait of the Canadian with that of the colonists of New England.

> One finds here no rich persons whatever, and this is a great pity; for the Canadians like to get the credit of their money,

[1] *Mandements des Evêques de Québec,* vol. i, p. 352; *Jugements et Dél.,* vol. i, pp. 77-78; *Duchesneau au Ministre,* 10 Nov., 1679, cited by Parkman, *op. cit.,* vol. viii, p. 183; C. G., xii, *et seq.,* 382, 384, cited by Eastman, *op. cit.,* p. 275.

[2] Denonville and Champigny to the Minister, 1688, *Colon. Docs.,* vol. ix, p. 398. " Public drinking must have been very common, for Denonville complained to the king that there were no end of wine shops. The king in consequence ordered that the number be reduced. In 1725 the number was fixed at two for each parish." (Gosselin, *Henri de Berniéres,* p. 119.)

[3] *Mémoire Addressé au Régent,* cited by Parkman, *op. cit.,* vol. viii, p. 181; *cf. Colon. Docs. N. Y.,* vol. ix, p. 273.

and scarcely anybody amuses himself with hoarding it. They say it is very different with our neighbors the English; and one who knew the two colonies by the way of living, acting, and speaking of the colonists would not hesitate to judge ours the more flourishing. . . . In New France poverty is hidden under an air of ease which appears entirely natural. . . . The French colonist enjoys what he has got, and often makes a display of what he has not got.[1]

Duchesneau, the *Intendant*, states that "all except five or six of the merchants and a small number of artisans are plunged in poverty because the vanity of the women and the debauchery of the men consume all their gains".[2]

Kalm, seventy years later, appears to have been of much the same opinion, for he says, "The Frenchmen who considered things in their true light, complained very much that a great part of the ladies in Canada had got into the pernicious custom of taking too much care of their dress, and squandering all their fortunes, and more, upon it, instead of sparing something for future times."[3]

It is true that there were many of the austere type[4] among the clergy and religious orders, as well as among the faithful of the laity; still, the mass of the people, although devoutly religious,[5] belonged to the forceful and

[1] Charlevoix, cited by Parkman, *Old Régime*, vol. ii, p. 195.

[2] *Duchesneau au Ministre,* 10 Nov., 1679, cited by Parkman, vol. viii, p. 183.

[3] Kalm, *op. cit.,* vol. iii, p. 281.

[4] Giddings, *Ind. Soc.*, p. 83; *cf. ibid., Hist. and Desc. Soc.*, pp. 230-231, 234, 236.

[5] "The French, in their colonies, spend much more time in prayer and external worship than the English and Dutch settlers in the British colonies. . . . The French here have prayers every morning and night on board their shipping, and on Sundays they pray more than commonly; they regularly say grace at their meals; and every one of them says prayers in private as soon as he gets up. At Fort *St. Frederic* all the soldiers assembled together for morning and evening prayers." (Kalm, vol. iii, pp. 43-44; *cf. Const. Docs.*, vol. i, p. 53; Stillman, *Remarks on Quebec*, p. 386.)

convivial groups; and any austerity of life which they assumed was very largely the result of isolation and the rigorous discipline of the church. This is very vividly brought out by Le Jeune when he writes:

I have here a request to make of all those who wish to express an opinion of the condition of our colony,—to close their eyes while the ships are at anchor in our ports, and to open them at their departure, or shortly afterwards, to the agreeable sight of our countrymen. They wish to make merry and they fall into excesses; their good habits grow drowsy, and vice begins to raise its head; there is a greater indulgence in drink and feasting during that time than in all the rest of the year. . . . But when the fleet has departed, when visits come to an end, when the winter begins to rally us, how they lend ear to the word of God, and how those who have taken too much liberty recognize their shortcomings! Then those who thought that lawlessness reigned in our colony joyfully praise the piety and devotion thereof . . . [1]

Although given to ostentation and display, and fond of honors and attentions,[2] they " were not wanting in many of the virtues of a simple and industrious life or those which common consent attributes to the nation from which they had sprung ".[3] While generally acknowledged to be litigious,[4] they were little given to offences against property,

[1] *Rel.* 1636-1637, vol. xi, p. 73.

[2] Munro, *Docs. S. T.*, p. xci.

[3] Durham, *op. cit.*, p. 17. Cf. " Though not slothful in business, they sought mainly to serve themselves, whom they esteemed the salt of the earth—a truculent conceit which was not, the intendant [Hocquart] thought, a useful handmaid to industrial, commercial or agricultural progress. Their enforced idleness in the long winter period was also, in his opinion, somewhat detrimental to industrious habits, especially since by nature they loved the chase and the roving life in general." (Munro, *op. cit.*, pp. xci-xcii.)

[4] Charlevoix, *op. cit.*, vol. iii, p. 190; *A Pol. and Hist. Account of L. C.*, p. 140.

or violence against the person;[1] rather, although naturally independent and self-assertive, were they held by common consent to be kindly and hospitable, virtuous and honest.[2]

They were largely of the ideo-emotional type of mind and less dogmatic-emotional than their descendants of to-day.[3] Cheerful and good-humored, they were distinguished for courtesy and politeness, and while not as lively and vivacious as their French ancestors, yet they were by no means dull.[4] Swayed largely by feeling, and under the control of the unquestioned authority of the church and state, reason had very little opportunity to assert itself. As they were shut off for most of the year from the outside world, conservatism and traditionalism prevailed.[5] "They clung to ancient prejudices, ancient customs, and ancient laws, not from any strong sense of their beneficial effects, but with the unreasoning tenacity of an uneducated and unprogressive people."[6]

It is very clear that traits of the sort described in the

[1] Charlevoix, *op. cit.*, vol. iii, p. 190; The Canadian French, *Massachusetts Bureau of Statistics of Labor*, 1882, p. 65.

[2] *Revolutionary Letters*, p. 31; *cf. Const. Docs.*, vol. i, p. 60; *Mass. B. of L.*, p. 52.

[3] Giddings, *Ind. Soc.*, pp. 84-87; *cf. ibid., Hist. and Disc. Soc.*, pp. 236-240.

[4] "A more good-humoured people than the latter (French Canadian) can hardly be found; but the sparkling vivacity, the vehemence of temper, the tiger-like passion and the brilliant fiery wit of a Frenchman are not to be found among them." (*A Pol. and Hist. Account of L. C.*, p. 141.) *Cf.* "Notwithstanding their poverty, they are always cheerful and in high spirits." (Kalm, vol. iii, p. 192.) *Cf.* "They will be out of doors talking and singing between themselves. They are just like the French in the Canadian villages. They like to sing, and they are a little noisy, but always friendly. . . ." (*Mass. B. of L.*, 1882, p. 54.)

[5] "The news of the day amounts to very little indeed, as the country furnishes scarcely any, while that from Europe comes all at once." (Charlevoix, cited by Parkman, vol. viii, p. 195.)

[6] Durham, *op. cit.* p. 17.

foregoing pages were such as to render the population as a whole readily amenable to ecclesiastical control. It is in the sphere of religion, however, that the greatest degree of homogeneity among the French Canadians was exhibited. The policy begun under Richelieu of a rigorous exclusion of Protestants, although it robbed the church of the stimulus which comes through criticism and the fear of proselytizing, had, nevertheless, been of primary importance for unity of faith and practice. Everywhere throughout New France there was uniformity of worship. There was one church and one religious leadership, under the supervision of a watchful bishop. The attendance at church represented the whole community as most of the people were to be found at the services. The presence, from almost the beginning, of a strong and relatively large group of clergy in the colony, backed by a highly organized church with rather liberal financial support, and in control of all education, gave to the church, in Quebec, stability and prestige; and at the same time, enabled it not only to maintain the ordinances of religion with dignity and fitting solemnity in the older parishes, but also to follow the people into the newer settlements and thus retain them within the fold.

The rigorous exclusion of Protestants from New France merely reflected the attitude of Roman Catholicism to Protestantism during the sixteenth and seventeenth centuries. "Excessive intolerance was inwrought in the moral sanctions of the period".[1] In no other country except The Netherlands was the struggle more bitter than in France.

From the beginning of French colonization in Canada, the evangelization of the natives was held to be the exclusive field of Roman Catholic missions. The Protestants seem to have accepted this situation, for De Monts, al-

[1] Reyss, *Étude sur quelques points de l'histoire de la tolérance au Canada et aux Antilles*, p. 8.

though a Huguenot,[1] requested the blessing of the pope on the mission among the natives.[2]

Among the early traders in New France the greater number were Huguenots, who while enjoying their trading privileges under a Roman Catholic government, were nevertheless strongly Protestant in their sympathies. Beneath the surface there was much the same bitterness as between the members of the two faiths in France.[3]

Notwithstanding the strong religious prejudices, however, the authorities of the earlier days appear to have carried out the spirit of the Edict of Nantes of 1598. De Monts, for example, provided both Protestant ministers and Roman Catholic priests; [4] and it is said that in 1603 he openly granted liberty of conscience to the Huguenots of his party.[5]

A like measure of religious tolerance was enjoyed for a time on the St. Lawrence.[6] Protestant traders early had found their way up the river.[7] In 1621 a strong company was organized and placed under the control of Guillaume

[1] *Champlain's Voyages*, The Publications of the Prince Society, vol. i, p. 35.

[2] "Inasmuch as his chief object is to establish the Christian religion in the land which his Majesty has been pleased to grant him and to lead to that faith the poor savage folk . . . he thought fit to ask the blessing of the Pope of Rome . . . by a formal letter." (Marc Lescarbot, *History of New France*, The Publications of the Champlain Society, vol. ii, p. 368.)

[3] Lescarbot relates that, when a young churchman was lost in the woods, "already they accused a certain man of the so-called Reformed religion of having murdered him, for they had more than one quarrel over the said religion." (*Ibid.*, vol. ii, p. 233.)

[4] *Ibid.*, vol. ii, p. 287.

[5] Brasseur de Bourbourg, *Histoire du Canada, de son église et ses missions*, p. 24.

[6] Salone, *La Colonisation de la Nouvelle-France*, p. 43.

[7] *Can. and its Prov.*, vol. ii, New France ii, pp. 450-451.

and Emery de Caën, two Protestant merchants of Rouen.[1] The religious influence of this company was soon viewed with apprehension by the Roman Catholic Fathers in the colony.[2] On the ground that this company had not fulfilled its charter obligations as regards colonization, a new company was formed, called the company of One Hundred Associates. This company, on the one hand, agreed to settle in the colony some sixteen thousand native-born French Catholics between the years 1628 and 1643, and, on the other hand, promised that care would be taken that no foreigner or heretic entered the country.[3]

In France, Richelieu's administration was beginning to give renewed unity and strength to the state. His policy aimed at the humiliation of the nobles, the overthrow of the Huguenots, and the restoration of the prestige of France. To achieve this end, he says, "I promised your Majesty to employ all my ability, and all the authority it should please you to delegate to me, in ruining the Huguenot party, in lowering the pride of the nobles, and in restoring your name to the position it should occupy among foreign nations." [4]

[1] *Can. and its Prov.*, vol. ii, New France ii, p. 451.

[2] "The Jesuits . . . soon realized that a colony founded for the spread of the Catholic religion could never prosper so long as it was at the mercy of a company managed by Calvinists seeking nothing but commercial gain." (*Ibid.*, p. 398.)

[3] *Edits et Ord.* (1803), vol. i, pp. 2-3; *cf.* also Charlevoix, vol. ii, pp. 38-39.

". . . . Without it being permitted to the said associates and others to send any foreigner to the said places, thus to populate the said colony with native French Catholics, and it will be ordered to those who command in New France to see to it that the present article is executed exactly according to its form and tenor, not suffering that it should be infringed upon for any cause or occasion whatsoever under pain of personal responsibility." (An Act establishing the Company of One Hundred Associates, April 29th, 1627, *Edits and Ord.*, vol. i, art. ii, p. 3.)

[4] Duruy, *History of France*, p. 392.

The exclusion of the Huguenots under the charter of the Company of One Hundred Associates, already mentioned, merely extended this avowed policy of Richelieu to Canada. The various explanations given—such as the existence at the court of a strong suspicion that the Calvinists had been guilty of an intrigue with the English against Canada,[1] or, again, Richelieu's determination that the awful struggle then going on before La Rochelle should be made forever impossible in the colony.[2] Such explanations, if true, only strengthen the conviction that the Protestants were excluded from New France as part of the great Cardinal's national policy.

The edict forbidding, under penalty, the admission of Protestants was, for a time, at least, strictly observed, and, in cases where Protestants were found living in Canada, severe pressure was brought to bear by the authorities to induce them to recant. Le Mercier's Journal of September 14, 1664, records with much satisfaction that more than twenty heretics had been converted.[3] Evidently there were other Protestants in the colony with whom their efforts to proselytize were less successful, for in the same year his Majesty was petitioned,

to select them from the Isle de France, Normandy, Picardy and to send over to New France families to settle the country, and the neighboring provinces, as the people there were, it was said, laborious, industrious, full of religious feeling, while the provinces near the seaports, where the shipments were

[1] Charlevoix, *op. cit.*, vol. ii, p. 67.

[2] Salone, *op. cit.*, p. 45.

[3] *Rel.*, vol. l, p. 85.

"His Majesty is glad to learn that there are no Protestants in Canada and that the soldiers who were still of the P. R. R. [Pretended Reformed Religion] have been converted." (*Colon. Docs. N. Y.*, vol. ix, p. 312; *cf. C. A.*, B. 74, pt. i, p. 50.)

made, contained many heretics, and a population less adapted to agriculture.[1]

In order that the Protestant traders who visited the St. Lawrence might not undermine the faith of their Roman Catholic brethren, they were prohibited from spending the winter in Canada.[2] Soldiers and workmen engaged in the king's service, however, were exempt from this restriction.[3]

Bishop Laval, in a memorial of 1670, urged that the French merchants should be prohibited from sending out Protestant clerks. He accused the clerks not only of holding religious meetings of their own, but of unsettling the faith of some Roman Catholics, both by their conversations and their habits of lending heretical books. The bishop further pointed out the danger of allowing the Protestants to increase in the colony, on the ground that they were

[1] Charlevoix, *op. cit.*, vol. iii, p. 81.

[2] Salone, *op. cit.*, p. 44.

[3] "This Wednesday, the twentieth of August, 1664:—The Council having met, there being present the Bishop, Messrs. de la Ferté and d'Auteüil, together with the *Procureur-Général* of the King:

"Touching the petition presented by Möise Hilleret and Daniel Beau, ship-carpenters, setting forth that their year of engagement had expired by the twenty-eighth of May last; and, furthermore, that they can not remain any longer in this country, unless the affairs of the King detain them here, inasmuch as they are of the so-called Reformed religion; [and asking] that they should be allowed to return to France this year; and that they may be paid for the three months of service which they have given over and above their year; and that their passage homeward be paid on their behalf;

"Having heard upon this matter the recommendations of the *Procureur-Général*, to the effect that the decree of the King's Council of State be carried out; and that, inasmuch as the year of the Petitioners has expired, they be sent back to France;

"The Council, in rendering judgment, has granted to the Petitioners the object of their requests for the purpose of their return; and has furthermore ordered that the same be put into effect at the earliest date." (*Jugements et Dél.*, vol. i, pp. 262-263.)

known to be less loyal than Roman Catholics, and their proximity to the English colonists would eventually lead to political discord.[1]

Despite, however, the watchful eye of the church, supported by the arm of the state, from time to time Protestants found their way into the colony. In reply to a request asking for the expulsion of the Protestants then resident in the colony, Beauharnois and Hocquart were informed in 1742 that "His Majesty is not willing to send back to France the individuals of the so-called Reformed religion who are in Canada, on the ground of what you write about their good conduct, but if later on something should happen on their part contrary to good order, it would be necessary to provide for it. You will take care to watch them."[2]

[1] "The Bishop of Quebec represents that the French merchants are sending out Protestant clerks (*commis*) and that for some time past the clergy have been pointing out the disadvantages [of this practice] with respect both to religion and to the State.

"As regards religion, the Bishop of Quebec affirms that they use much seductive language; that they lend books, and that, at times, they have even held meetings together; and that, finally, he has knowledge that many persons speak highly of them, and are unable to believe that they [the Protestants] are in error.

"When this matter is examined in its relation to the State, it is evident that its importance is equally great [there]. It is common knowledge that the Protestants in general are not as attached to His Majesty as are the Catholics.

"Quebec is not very far removed from Boston and other English towns, and to multiply the Protestants in Canada would be to provide a future cause of disorder. Those who are here have not appeared to show an especially sympathetic interest in the success of His Majesty's arms; and they have been observed to show some eagerness in spreading abroad the news of all the trifling reverses which have occurred.

"An order forbidding French merchants to send over Protestant clerks will be sufficient to put an end to this abuse." (Memoirs of the Bishop of Quebec regarding Protestants, 1670, *Collection de Manuscrits . . . (de) la Nouvelle-France*, vol. i, pp. 204-205.)

[2] *C. A.*, B, vol. 74, pt. i, p. 250.

Evidently, nothing did happen contrary to good order, for when the country passed into the hands of the British, seventeen years later, there were some few still living in Canada who had been able to withstand the opposition of the Catholic church.[1] General Murray took a deep interest in these, maintaining that if the government were to provide a church and minister for them, they might be able to induce many of their persecuted brethren in France to emigrate to Canada. In this way, he believed, the government might build up a strong Huguenot community which would tend to lessen the prejudice of the people against the Protestant faith.[2]

It is clear, however, that the few Protestants who found their way into New France, from time to time, never were in a position either politically or numerically to organize in any way for purposes of religious worship. Catholicism was not only master of the religious field, but had it completely to itself. Uniformity of worship prevailed in all the parishes, and, except in a few of the larger centres, all the people worshiped in the same church.

The clergy, when compared with the conditions prevailing where Catholicism and Protestantism exist side by side, presented an undivided leadership. Divisions and jealousies seem to have been common among the religious orders. The Jesuits, although coming to Canada at the invitation of the *Récollets*, had no sooner landed than they began to usurp the place so worthily held by their brothers of the Order of St. Francis. The warning which Le Clercq says had reached the ears of the *Récollets*, that the Jesuits

[1] Maseres' statement that "there were only three Protestant families" among the French Canadians at the time of the conquest seems doubtful. *Cf. Const. Docs.*, vol. i, p. 179.

[2] General Murray's report on the state of the government of Quebec, June 5th, 1762. *Const. Docs.* vol. i, p. 54.

would not be satisfied until they were first, was soon shown to be true. In a brief time they had supplanted the *Récollets*,[1] and were in a position to dominate the policy of the church in New France. Under Laval the religious leadership was still further unified; in the first place through ousting the appointee of the Archbishop of Rouen, the Sulpician vicar-general Queylus, and in the second place, by bringing about the erection of the bishopric of Quebec directly subject to the See of Rome.

The religious leadership in New France was not only strongly centralized, but was also of such a character and strength as to meet adequately the needs of the colony. Its members, as represented both by the religious orders of *Récollets*, Jesuits, and Sulpicians, and by individuals such as Caron, Lalemont, Queylus, and Laval, were not only austere and persevering, but at the same time able and devoted.[2]

Laval, although undoubtedly the ablest, was nevertheless typical of that group of austere and persevering churchmen who laid the foundations of Catholicism in New France. He had received his training in the colleges of La Fléche and Clermont, both under the direction of the Jesuits.[3] After leaving the college he spent four years in the Hermitage at Caen, under one Berniers, a zealous supporter of the ultramontane teachings of the Jesuits in their struggle against the Jansenist doctrines. This band of zealots held it as as their duty to be the guardians of sound doctrine, and to this end watched every pulpit in the city for signs of Jansenism. Austere in their habits of life,

[1] Kingsford, William, *History of Canada*, vol. i, p. 122 *et seq.*

[2] Parkman, *The Jesuits in North America*, vol. i, p. 131.

[3] Leblond de Brumath, Bishop Laval, *The Makers of Canada*, p. 19; *cf.* also *Can. and its Prov.*, vol. ii, N. F. ii, p. 418.

they were exceedingly dogmatic in their religious teaching.[1] It was in this atmosphere of asceticism and mysticism, of annihilation of self and absorption in God, that the character of Laval was moulded.[2]

From almost the very beginning of the colony, liberal provision was made for the spiritual oversight of the French and the Indians. From four ecclesiastics in 1615, the number had been increased to twenty-nine in 1640, not including the six nuns who were at work in Quebec. In 1650, the Jesuits alone numbered forty with a like number of servants.[3] The clergy had increased to fifty-one in 1665, and comprised one bishop, eighteen priests and ecclesiastics, and thirty-one Jesuit priests and brethren, while the nuns numbered forty-six, including nineteen Ursulines, twenty-three of the Hospitaller order, and four *filles pieuses* of the congregation.[4] In 1685 the number classed as ecclesiastical persons was 179, and they included the bishop, thirty-six priests, and fourteen other ecclesiastics, forty-three Jesuits, eleven *Récollets,* twenty-eight Ursulines, thirty-six hospital sisters, and ten other women who had taken a religious vow.[5] In the same year the total Indian and French population was given as 12,263, of whom 1,538 were Christian Indians settled in villages, and 10,725 were French or Canadian-born whites.[6] Exactly what proportion of these ecclesiastical persons ministered to this resident Indian and French population is not easily ascertained, since a considerable number were engaged in the Indian missions beyond.

[1] Parkman, *Old Régime*, p. 88 *et seq.*

[2] *Ibid.*, p. 167.

[3] Sulte, *R. S. C. Trans.*, 1905, sec. ii, p. 112.

[4] *Census* 1665.

[5] *Mémoires sur le Canada*, p. 167.

[6] *Census* 1685.

When we come to consider the rural parishes, we find that there was one parish to every 220, or less, of the rural population, for we know that there were forty rural parishes, each having a curé, and that the total rural population was 8,796.[1] The total Indian and white population was even smaller, having one curé to every 166 persons. In 1719, with a population of 22,530, there were 333 ecclesiastical persons, including sixteen Jesuits, twelve *Récollets,* fifty-one parish priests, and eighteen priests in the seminaries, fifty Ursulines, 106 Hospitallers, sixty-eight nuns of the congregation, and twelve from the General Hospital.[2] In 1754, there were 380 ecclesiastical persons ministering to a population of 55,009; 155 of whom were male, and 255 female. The number of priests in the rural parishes had increased to ninety-one; but, as the rural population was 42,000, the ratio of priests to population was less than half of that in 1681, being one priest to every 463.[3]

Liberal provision also was made in New France for the support of the religious institutions. Of the land granted by the French king in the colony, 2,043,790 acres were in ecclesiastical hands; the Jesuits were the largest holders, with 881,695 acres; the Ursulines held 551,712 acres; the Sulpicians, 196,367 acres; the Seminary of Quebec, 161,-622 acres; and the hospitals and other similar institutions, 56,925.[4] The king's gifts in money were equally generous. The church in New France received the larger part of the funds known as the "ordinary charges" of the colony. Out of an appropriation of 36,360 *livres* for the year 1667, 28,000 was assigned for religious purposes; the Jesuits re-

[1] *Census* 1681.

[2] *Census* 1719.

[3] *Census* 1754.

[4] *C. A.*, Q. 56, pt. iii, p. 833.

ceiving 6,000 *livres*; the Ursulines, 6,000 *livres*; the cathedral, 9,000; the Seminary, 4,000; and the Hotel-Dieu, 3,000. In 1689, the total amount had increased to 34,000 *livres,* including the sums assigned to Acadia.[1] In a letter dated May 5, 1700, from the minister to the bishop, the former states that "His Majesty has been pleased to continue the fund of 8,000 *livres* for the support of the curés."[2] The king evidently considered the money well spent, for the minister says, "the report given by them, and by you, of the number of the curés who have been more permanent, and of the good use made of this sum last year, has induced him to continue the fund." The king, however, did not intend this grant to be more than temporary. He still hoped "that, as soon as the land has again become productive, as in the past, and when more of it is brought under cultivation, the tithes will be sufficient to support them," and in order to bring this about as soon as possible, he instructed two of his officers "to devise with you [the bishop] means to place the tithes in a condition to support the curés in the future."[4] The bishopric of Quebec was endowed by him with the revenues of two, and later three, French Abbeys.[5]

[1] Parkman, *Old Régime*, p. 336.

[2] The Minister to Bishop of Quebec, 5th May, 1700; *C. A.*, Moreau St. Méry, F3, vol. vi, p. 78.

[3] *Ibid.*

[4] *Ibid.*

[5] Parkman, *Old Régime*, p. 337. *Cf.* "And for the suitable support of the Bishop of Quebec, while holding office, we do set apart the revenue of the Board of the Monastery of the Abbey called de Millebecco (of the Order of Saint Benedict), in the diocese of Bituruca, which is wont to be called *incommendam*, which the said Francis obtained lately and holds to-day *incommendam;* and the joint collate, title and designation of abbot, with all right of nomination thereto (to the abbey), which in virtue of agreements long since made between the

The king's generosity called forth other large private benefactions. Various members of the court, in the few years following 1636, contributed more than 75,000 *livres*. Charitable ladies gave largely to the hospital and other good works; Madame Bullion's donations alone amounted to 20,000 *livres* in the year 1646,[1] and altogether to 62,000 *livres*.[2]

The revenues derived from the colonists for the maintenance of religious ordinances were, however, less satisfactory. The Company of One Hundred Associates, according to their charter, were to provide for the maintenance of three curés in each of their settlements.[3] After the

said Apostolic See and Francis I, of illustrious memory, at one time king of the said French, belongs to the aforesaid King Louis, we do, with the consent of the aforesaid King Louis, and with reservation to our beloved sons, the Prior and Monks of the conventual Board and all spiritual jurisdiction within the limits of the said Monastery, suppress and extinguish for ever by the same authority; and with the consent of the same King Louis, we do, by our oft-named Apostolic authority, for ever assign to, unite with, and incorporate in the same church of Quebec and its episcopal Board, the said Monastery, along with all its rights, jurisdictions, revenues and emoluments, and we do grant and assign to the future Bishop of Quebec himself the aforesaid state as his State, and, as his diocese the lands, towns, and places in the aforesaid district, as they at present exist for the time being under the temporal dominion of the said King Louis, to be now subject to the spiritual jurisdiction of no other bishop—according to the boundaries to be marked by the same King Louis and approved by the aforesaid Apostolic See—and the community and people of the City of Quebec and of its lands, towns and places, and the communities, residents and inhabitants of the said district as his people, and belonging to his diocese, and their ecclesiastics as his clergy." (Bull, Erecting the Archbishopric of Quebec, *Mandements*, vol. i, p. 82 *et seq.*)

[1] *Mémoires sur le Canada*, pp. 138-139.

[2] Charlevoix, *op. cit.*, vol. iii, p. 27.

[3] "In each settlement which shall be established by the said associates, in order to look after the conversion of the Indians and the consolation of the French who will reside in the said New France, there will

withdrawal of the company's charter in 1663, the Seminary of Quebec undertook to furnish curés for the colony, and, in return was to receive all the tithes,[1] which were then fixed at one-thirteenth.[2] For the next seventy years the tithes were a source of controversy and dispute.

Education, under the French régime, was almost altogether in the hands of the church. The Jesuits were the first to establish a school. Father Le Jeune wrote, in 1635,

be three ecclesiastics at least whom the said associates will be obliged to provide with lodgings, provisions, ornaments, and furnish them generally with all things necessary, as well for their living as for the functions of their ministry, during the said fifteen years, unless the said associates, in order to avoid the said expenses, prefer to distribute to the said ecclesiastics cleared lands sufficient for their support. Even there will be sent to the said New France a greater number of ecclesiastics if need be and if the company deems it advisable either for the said settlements or for the missions; the whole at the expense of the said associates during the period of the said fifteen years; and those being expired, His Majesty will hand over the surplus to the devotion and charity as well of those of the said company as of the French who will reside there, who will be exhorted to provide abundantly as well for the said ecclesiastics as for all others who will go to New France in order to work for the salvation of souls." (*Edits. et Ord.* (1803), vol. i, p. 3, art. iii.)

[1] "It is absolutely necessary to provide the said Seminary and clergy with a sufficient revenue to meet the outlays and the expenses which it will be obliged to make. We have applied and do apply, have affected and do affect, from the present and for all time, all tithes of whatever nature they may be, and in the way in which they will be levied in all parishes and places of the said country, to be held in common and administered by the said seminary according to our orders and our authority, and of the successor of the bishops of the country, on the condition that he will furnish the maintenance of all the ecclesiastics who will be assigned to the parishes and other places of the said country, and who will always be removable, and subject to the recall at the will of the said bishops and seminary by their orders." (*Edits et Ord.* (1803), vol. i p. 26.)

[2] The edict ordered that "the tithes shall be paid on everything produced by the labour of man, and on everything which the earth produces by the labour of man." (*Ibid.*, p. 314.)

that a building had been erected near the fort, and that the children were being instructed.[1] The *Récollets* who had done some preliminary educational work among the Indians before the arrival of the Jesuits, conducted a successful school at Quebec, which was said to have had more students than that of the Jesuits.[2] The Sulpicians opened a school for boys, in 1657, at Montreal.[3] Twenty-one years later, in 1686, the "Association of the Citizens of Montreal for Schools" was formed and placed under the direction of this order. Three of the four teachers employed by the Association were ecclesiastics.[4]

There were thirty-two primary schools for boys established during the French period in New France, fifteen of which were situated in the city and district of Quebec, ten in the city and district of Montreal, and seven in the town and district of Three Rivers.[5] The education of girls was provided by fifteen different institutions; nine of which were convents, and six houses of education. The convents were to be found in different parts of the country, as well as in Montreal and Quebec. Three of the houses of education were in Quebec, one in Montreal, and two in Three Rivers.[6] The two leading orders engaged in educational work for girls were the Ursulines, and the Sisters of the Congregation of Notre-Dame.[7]

The School of Mathematics and Hydrography, founded about 1665 at Quebec, was the only one of the fifty-four

[1] Gosselin, Amédée E., *L'Instruction au Canada*, pp. 33-34.

[2] *Mémoires sur le Canada*, p. 86.

[3] Gosselin, *op. cit.*, p. 79.

[4] *Ibid.*, p. 82.

[5] *Ibid.*, pp. 475-476.

[6] *Ibid.*, p. 477.

[7] *Ibid.*, pp. 144-169.

educational institutions not under the direction and control of the church. This school was established and maintained by the king, and was under the direction of the "master of hydrography for the King at Quebec."[1] The Jesuits were eager to get control of this school, but, for a time, had to content themselves with giving lessons in mathematics.[2] On the death of the master of the school, Jolliet, in 1707, the Jesuits carried on the work, and in the following year, the direction and control of the school, with its revenues, passed into their hands.[3] In Montreal they had been able to control this branch of education[4] from the very beginning.

The proportion of the school population reached by these various educational institutions seems to have been small; although the schools were fairly numerous considering the size of the population. The official census of 1685 showed that there were 10,725 French and 1,538 Indians in New France, not including Acadia.[5] At this date, nineteen educational institutions had been established, or one for every 645 of the population. Very few of these, however, were outside of Montreal and Quebec.[6] And in most of these, during the seventeenth century, the instruction given was very elementary. In a letter to His Majesty, suggesting that he make a grant for the support of an instructor in geometry, fortification, and geography, it was stated that "At Montreal the youth is deprived of all education. The children go to the public schools, which are established at

[1] Gosselin, *op. cit.*, pp. 331, 345.

[2] *Ibid.*, p. 333.

[3] *Ibid.*, p. 337.

[4] *Ibid.*, p. 334.

[5] *Mémoires sur le Canada*, p. 167.

[6] Gosselin, pp. 475-477; *Can. and its Prov.*, vol. xvi, pp. 347, 350.

the Seminary of St. Sulpice, and with the Brothers Charon, where they learn the first elements of grammar only."[1] Social rank does not appear to have made much difference, for it was said, "All the education which the children of the officers and of the gentry receive is very slight, they can hardly read and write. They do not know the primary elements of geography and history, and it is much to be desired that they have more education."[2]

In the programme of studies for elementary schools, religion had the first place. It was considered of the greatest importance, and essential as a foundation for all education.[3]

Thus it is seen that in the field of education the church was in control of the school, the most powerful instrument of standardization;[4] and that not only was there no competition from other religious bodies, but, except for the School of Hydrography, all education which consisted of religious instruction was absolutely in the hands of the church.

The ability with which the church, under British rule, was still able to dominate education, notwithstanding the opposition of both the government and the Protestants, had an even more significant effect upon the rise of ecclesiastical control.

This supremacy, after the conquest, seemed in grave danger of being assumed by the state and the Church of England. By the articles of capitulation, the male teaching orders, who were in practical control of education, were not to be preserved in their constitution and privileges,

[1] *Mémoires sur le Canada*, p. 209.

[2] *Ibid.*, p. 208.

[3] Gosselin, *op. cit.*, p. 227.

[4] *Can. and its Prov.*, vol. xvi, Q. ii, pp. 348-350.

until the king's pleasure should be known.[1] By the Treaty of Paris, in 1763, these restrictions were confirmed, their property passed into the hands of the crown, and they were forbidden to receive any new members into their orders.[2]

The belief, which seems to have been warranted, that these estates were to be alienated from the support of education,[3] raised a storm of protest. Petitions signed by both the clergy and laity were forwarded to the governor and council requesting the continuance of the religious orders, and the restoration of their property for educational purposes.[4] The matter was brought to the attention of the Colonial Office, for Hillsborough wrote to Carleton in these terms: "Upon this subject I have little else to say than that the consideration of what may be finally proper and expedient in respect to that is still before his Majesty's

[1] Articles of Capitulation between General Amherst and Marquis de Vaudreuil, *Annual Register*, 1760, art. xxxiii, p. 222.

[2] "You are not to allow the admission of any new members into any of the said societies or Communities, the Religious Communities of Women only excepted, without Our express orders for that purpose. That the society of Jesuits be suppressed and dissolved, and no longer continued, as a Body corporate and politic, and all their Rights, Possessions and Property shall be vested in Us for such purposes, as We may hereafter think fit to direct and appoint; but We think fit to declare Our Royal Intention to be, that the present members of the said Society as established at Quebec shall be allowed sufficient stipends and Provisions during their natural lives." (Instructions to Governor Carleton, 1775, *C. A.*, Q. 26b, p. 139.)

[3] "Their estate might be put under proper management, and such of their lands, which are the very best in the country, as are unconceded, might be let to English farmers (encouraged on purpose to introduce a better notion of husbandry and to mix with the people); the produce of the whole to be applied to defray the expenses." (*C. A.*, Q. 1, p. 253; Q. 84, pp. 291-292.)

[4] *C. A.*, Q. 6, pp. 115, 117; Q. 7, pp. 368-371; *C. A.*, P. C.—H., p. 449; Q. 35, pp. 66-70, 70-106, 110-116.

Privy Council. . . . My Lord President [of Board of Trade] has given reason to believe that it will now immediately be taken up." [1]

Public opinion, both Roman Catholic and Protestant became strongly averse to any scheme tending to alienate these lands from education, either by granting them to Lord Amherst, or having them appropriated for the province. Dorchester wrote to Sydney that,

In consequence of some steps taken in obedience to His Majesty's Order in Council of the 18th August 1786 respecting the Grant to be made to Lord Amherst of the estates formerly held by the Jesuits in this province, a petition was presented by a considerable number of respectable inhabitants, accompanied by a memorial setting forth that the greatest part of the said estates originated from private donations of individuals made for the express purpose of constituting a fund for the education of youth under the name of the college of Quebec, that the same ought to be considered as the property of the public and not to be diverted from that channel, and praying that the necessary measures may be taken to apply the said estates accordingly for the support of such an institution which has long been talked of and is very much wanted in this province. . . . The said petition is now under consideration, and shall be transmitted to your Lordship by another opportunity.[2]

The Anglican clergy were as eager as their Roman Catholic brethren that the Jesuit estates should be used to promote education, and addressed a petition to the Bishop of Nova Scotia, praying that, since the lands had been granted originally for purposes of education and in view of the need,

[1] *C. A.*, Q. 6, p. 121.

[2] Dorchester to Sydney, Dec. 10, 1787; *C. A.*, Q. 35, p. 1; Q. 49, p. 21.

the property should be used in the widest interests of education in the province.[1]

Considering the backward state of education at this period among the masses in England, it was not to be expected that the government would be keenly alive to the needs of education in Quebec. Such pressure, nevertheless, was brought to bear by both old and new subjects that, in 1786, a committee was appointed by the King's Order in Council to investigate and report upon the Jesuits' estates in order to enable the governor " to adjust the quantum to be reserved for public uses and to determine the parcels

[1] " Right Revd. Sir:

" We, your clergy of the Province of Quebec, whose names are underwritten, take the liberty of addressing you on a subject which gives the most flattering prospects of general utility to this His Majesty's Province.

" The original grant of what are called the Jesuit lands, being destined, as we understand, for the education of youth, gives us hopes that the intent of the pious donors may not be frustrated, and further emboldens us to supplicate His Majesty for the disposal of their lands in the behalf of knowledge and literature.

" We, who from our situation have the best opportunities of being acquainted with the real estate of the morals and dispositions of His Majesty's subjects in the different parts of this Province, have but too great cause to lament the want of a similar institution, and it is not for ourselves that we claim an exclusive property in such a blessing, but hope that the doors of learning may be open to all, and that the good effects of it may be as widely diffused as the religion we profess, to all ranks of men of whatever sect and nation of which this province is composed.

We are, Right Revd. Sir, Etc.,

Signed.
David Francis de Montmollin,
Philip Toosey,
Dd. Chd. Delisle,
John Doty,
James Tunstall,
Jno. Stuart,
John Langhorn,
L. Veyssière."

(*C. A.*, Q. 43, pt. ii, pp. 602-605.)

that might be disposed of . . ."[1] The report of this committee was, however, considered so unsatisfactory by Lord Dorchester, that no action was taken, although the appointment of the commission in itself indicated clearly that the government recognized the justice of their petitioners' claim.[2]

The chief difficulty in the way lay not so much in retaining these estates, for the support of education, as in uniting upon a scheme acceptable at once to the two races and the two religions.

There was, on the one hand, no doubt as to the deplorable state of education in the province.[3] The male portion of the population especially seems to have been sadly neglected.[4] Hugh Finlay wrote, in 1784, that,

> although the Canadian Peasants are far from being a stupid race, they are at present an ignorant people, from want of instruction. Not a man in five hundred among them can read; perhaps it has been the Policy of the Clergy to keep them in the dark, as it is a favorite tenet with the Roman Catholic Priests, that ignorance is the mother of devotion. The females in this country have great advantage over the males in point of education. The sisters of the congregation, or Grey Sisters as they are called, are settled in the Country Parishes here and there to teach girls to read, write, sew, and knit stockings.[5]

On the other hand, the desire of the government to have English become the language of the new subjects,[6] and the

[1] Dorchester to Grenville, *C. A.*, Q. 43, pt. ii, p. 593. [2] *Ibid.*

[3] *C. A.*, M. 914, p. 199; Q. 43, pt. i, p. 598; M. 128, p. 347; *Can. and its Prov.*, vol. xvi, Q. 2, p. 406.

[4] *C. A.*, Q. 10, p. 56 *et seq.*

[5] *C. A.*, Q. 23, pp. 441-442.

[6] *C. A.*, Q. 84, pp. 188, 293 and 294.

fear that the young men, in going to the revolted colonies for their classical training, might have their political principles "corrupted",[1] resulted in a committee's being appointed to consider the whole problem of elementary and secondary education.[2] In November, 1789, this committee, composed of five Protestants and four Roman Catholics, recommended, in a unanimous report, that there should be erected parish or village free schools throughout the province, tuition being allowed only for reading, writing, and ciphering; that there should be established a free secondary school in the central or county town of each district and,

that it is expedient to erect a collegiate institution, for cultivating the liberal arts and sciences usually taught in European universities, the theology of Christians excepted, on account of the mixture of the two communions whose joint aid is desirable as far as they agree, and who ought to be left to find a separate provision for candidates in the ministry of their respective churches. That it is essential to the origin and success of such an institution that a society be incorporated for the purpose, and that the charter wisely provide against the perversion of the institution to any sectarian peculiarities, leaving free scope for the cultivating of the general circle of the sciences.[3]

The report of the committee on education, while unanimous, was largely the product of Bishop Inglis,[4] and there-

[1] *C. A.*, Q. 43, pt. ii, p. 597; Q. 84, p. 186.

[2] *Can. and its Prov.*, vol. xvi, Q. 2, p. 447.

[3] *C. A.*, P. C.—G., p. 243; *cf. Can. and its Prov.*, vol. xvi, Q. 2, p. 447.

[4] "I shall only observe further on this head that the report had lain dormant since May 31, 1787, when Lord Dorchester had given an order on the subject; and would probably have continued so to this time had it not been for the exertion and stir I made last summer in this matter. I drew up and presented to Lord Dorchester a set of regulations for Canadian schools, July 22nd, and held a conference on the subject with

fore represented far more the Protestant than the Roman Catholic point of view. It had, however, the result of bring- the question of education before the people, and of making the Roman Catholic hierarchy declare itself.

To any one to-day, with even a slight knowledge of the history of education in Quebec, the scheme must appear an ambitious one, but at no time since does there seem to have been an occasion more opportune for a settlement of the vexed problem of education in a way that would have meant much for the future of Quebec and of Canada.

Bishop Inglis, himself, was doubtful of its success, for in April, 1790, he wrote to Dorchester, "I know it is your Lordship's wish to unite the Canadians with the Protestants in this design; and certainly this wish is dictated by benevolence and good policy—the question is—Can it be effected? I very much doubt it, in the present state of things." [1]

There were those in both the Protestant and Roman Catholic ranks who approved of the scheme and were eager to see it carried out.[2] All the Protestant clergy seem to have considered it a step in the right direction.[3] Although the ex-

several Canadian Magistrates and gentlemen, August 11th. The Legislative Council met and took some steps in this business the 13th of August, which produced this report the November following." (*C. A.*, M. 914, p. 197; *ibid.*, p. 51.)

[1] *C. A.*, M. 914, p. 199.

[2] *Ibid.*, p. 198.

[3] *C. A.*, Q. 49, pp. 26-29. *Cf.* "The Council of Quebec have taken so much time to make their report on the means of promoting education, I presume they have maturely weighed every circumstance. The plan seems to be very good—the only thing wanted is to realize it. In carrying on any measure here, I find that celerity in the execution is essential to its success. I am sensible that difficulties occur in Canada which are not easily surmounted, especially in this matter. . . . The guarding so scrupulously against 'the theology of Christians' being taught in the future college of Quebec, can proceed only from a jealousy that is groundless, and from not knowing the state of the Universities in Great Britain and Ireland. Attention to, and progress in, the sciences are the only things required in those Universities to qualify

clusion of the teaching of theology seems to have been disappointing to some, Mr. Bailly, Coadjutor to Bishop Hubert, came out strongly in favor of the plan against Bishop Hubert and the larger part of the Catholic clergy. So bitter was Bailly's criticism of Bishop Hubert's letter to the Committee on Education, that Dorchester did not think it proper for the government to publish it.[1]

What degree of support the Coadjutor had among the Roman Catholic laity seems difficult to ascertain. It must have been considerable, for Bishop Inglis, in April, 1790, wrote to Dorchester that he had received a letter from Quebec, lamenting "the ignorance and bigotry which prevail and are daily gaining ground among the Roman Catholics, and the separation which is kept up between them and the Protestants" and which the author wishes to be removed; it states that those Roman Catholics who possess liberal sentiments are discouraged, and injured, that this is particu-

the students for academical degrees. Theology is not forced upon any. There are, indeed, professors of Divinity; but none attend their Theological lectures except such as chuse it. There is no compulsion in the case; and it may be well enough to gratify the Canadians in this point." (*C. A.*, M. 914, p. 187.)

[1] "The letter of Monsieur Hubert of the 18th November, 1789, to the Chairman of the Committee on the subject of education, which was printed with their report, has been severely censured by the Coadjutor, Mr. Bailly, in a letter to the same Committee, which came too late to be inserted in their report, but was brought forward by them in a subsequent one, advising it to be published in the same manner as that of Monsieur Hubert.

"However, it did not seem decent for the government to become the channel of publishing their religious disputes, nor advisable even to afford an appearance for the suspicion of a wish to foment them.

"There is reason to suppose a much wider breach between them than could have been occasioned by a mere diversity of sentiment on the subject of Education. I have tried to reconcile them, but without effect. The clergy in general seem inclined to side with Monsieur Hubert." (Dorchester to Grenville, Nov. 10, 1790, *C. A.*, Q. 49, pp. 24-25.)

larly the case of Mr. Bailly, the Coadjutor. . . .[1] The writer even proposed, in order to overcome the reactionary attitude of Bishop Hubert, "to divide the Bishopric of Quebec into two Sees; to place Mr. Bailly immediately in one of them; and a native of His Majesty's European dominions, a Roman Catholic, in the other." [2]

No division of the bishopric was made however. Bishop Hubert was not forced to retire. The Roman Catholic hierarchy still retained control of education. Both the Government and the Church of England realized their defeat. The matter of the Jesuit estates was left in abeyance and the government sought other sources of revenue for the support of free schools.[3]

Bishop Hubert's attitude became the settled policy of the hierarchy. Notwithstanding the attempt of the Royal Institution for the Advancement of Learning of 1801 which made provision that the school should be "under the immediate inspection of the clergy of that religion which is possessed by the inhabitants of the spot—or where the inhabitants are of a mixed description, the clergy of each church

[1] *C. A.*, M. 914, p. 199. [2] *Ibid.*

[3] "The public having, according to the Tenor of your Grace's Dispatch No. 7 of the 12th of July last, been informed by my speech to both Houses of the Legislature that His Majesty has been graciously pleased to give directions for the establishing of a competent number of Free Schools, which has had the happiest effect in setting aside all reference to the Jesuits' Estates.

"The House of Assembly, so far from hinting at the subject of those . . . Estates either in their address or since, are now preparing a Bill for the purpose of seconding the beneficent views of His Majesty by erecting School Houses in the different parishes to be under the Control of the Executive Government; and should the Roman Catholic Clergy not use their influence in opposition to the measure, it will probably be adopted; but they seem to have hitherto discouraged the introduction of learning into the Province." Milne to Portland, Feb., 1801. (*C. A.*, Q. 84, pp. 272-273, 292-294; *cf.* Q. 85, pp. 376, 243; Q. 86, pt. i, p. 96; Q. 86, pt. ii, p. 372; Q. 88, p. 85.)

shall have the superintendence over the children of their respective communions,"[1] the Roman Catholic clergy refused to act as school visitors. The hierarchy tenaciously held to its policy that an educational system, to be acceptable to it, must recognize not only the denominational right to teach, but that such instruction must be under an educational department composed exclusively of Roman Catholics under the direction of their bishop.[2] This was obtained a few years later by placing the control of Roman Catholic education in the hands of the church.[3]

Thus the position of the Roman Catholic church now became much stronger than under the French régime; for not only had the church control of education, but indirectly, through the taxing power of the *fabriques*,[4] she was able to assess her people for the propagation of the Roman Catholic faith in the parish schools.

The social and moral solidarity, which has been emphasized in this chapter, made the French Canadian population as clay in the hands of the ecclesiastical potter.[5] The conservatism and traditionalism of such a homogeneous agricultural type of mind on the one hand rendered the people willingly obedient to the unquestioned authority of the church, while on the other, the barrier of language and the censorship of the hierarchy shut out everything tending to question this authority of the church. It is not surprising

[1] *Can. and its Prov.*, vol. xvi, Q. 2, pp. 450-455; *cf.* An Act for the Establishment of Free schools and the Advancement of Learning in this Province, *Anno quadragesimo primo Georgii*, III, 1801, *Laws of Lower Canada*, 1793-1804, vol. iii, p. 128.

[2] *Can. and its Prov., op. cit.*, vol. xvi, Q. 2, pp. 409-410.

[3] *Ibid.*, vol. xvi, Q. 2, pp. 412-413; *cf.* An Act to Facilitate the Establishment and Endowment of Elementary Schools in the Parishes of this Province, *Anno Quarto Georgii*, IV, 1824, *Laws of Lower Canada*, 1821-1824, p. 684.

[4] A council for the financial administration of a parish.

[5] *Cf.* Blackmar and Gillen, *Outlines of Sociology*, p. 350.

therefore that the church, thus strongly organized and adequately supported, unchallenged by any rival, religious or secular, except the state, should have been able to strengthen its influence and centralize its control. The possession of this immense centralized control, as the subsequent chapters show, not only brought the church into a conflict with the state but, of necessity, tended to a jealous guardianship of that control itself on the part of church authorities.

PART II

CHURCH AND STATE

CHAPTER IV

The Church and State in the French Period

The foregoing chapters have laid the sociological basis for explaining in some measure at least why it was that ecclesiastical control became so dominant in Quebec. They have made plain, to some extent at all events, that the situation, natural resources, population factors, occupations, language, social organization, psychological characteristics of the inhabitants, religious and educational institutions, of the region now included in the Province of Quebec were all conducive to the production of a remarkably homogeneous population and a well-developed mental and moral solidarity. It remains to trace in further detail the historical development of ecclesiastical control, and to show somewhat fully the precise ways in which the demographic and social factors heretofore considered reacted in that process up to the time of the Constitutional Act (1791).

The evolution of ecclesiastical control in Quebec, historically considered, falls naturally into two main periods; first the years from the settlement of the region down to the conquest by the British, and second the years from the conquest to the passing of the Constitutional Act. In both periods interest centres largely in the relation of Church and State. In both periods the power of the church was greatly increased in the process of adjusting the relationships of the church and state. The factors involved in the two periods, however, differed materially. In the first period there was but one religious faith to be taken into consideration; in the second the Church of England entered to complicate matters. In the first period the governmental officials were personally of the Roman Catholic faith and there was comparatively little reason for religious antagonism. In the second period not only were the governmental officials Protestant but the policies of the government itself were often opposed to what the Roman Catholic church considered its best interests. The officials were naturally somewhat more sympathetic with the aims of the Church of England than they were with those of the Roman Catholic hierarchy. Nevertheless in both periods the underlying demographic and social conditions remained relatively uniform. In the main it was these conditions which determined the outcome. Neither the personal characteristics of the rulers nor the change of political allegiance were sufficient at any time to overcome altogether the power of the Roman Catholic church. In fact the development of ecclesiastical control by the Roman Catholic church in the second period was more consistent than in the first, inasmuch as that control for some eighty years previous to the conquest showed a marked decline.

It is the purpose of this and the following chapters to trace the record of this evolution in detail. The present chapter will deal with the French period; the following one with the English period down to and including the Constitutional Act, as it affected both the Protestant and Roman Catholic churches, and the final chapter will include the summary and conclusion.

The foundation for the dominance of the church in Quebec was laid by two important preliminary facts—first, the religious motive in the exploration and colonization of New France,[1] and, second, the faithful work of the *Récollets*.

[1] The planting of the cross on the Gaspé Coast by Jacques Cartier was as significant for establishing the right of the Roman Catholic faith as the right of the French King. Cartier's purpose, in this initial

act of France in Canada, was to impress the natives with its religious significance; for he says: "After it [the cross] was raised in the air, we fell on our knees, with hands joined, while adoring it, before them, and made them signs, looking up and showing them the sky, that it was for our redemption." (*First Voyage of Jacques Cartier*, Dodd, Mead & Co., N. Y., 1906, p. 112.) The desire of Cartier to point the natives to the cross was characteristic of an age of religious enthusiasm both in government and people. Next to the passion for territorial aggrandizement was the pious wish to convert the heathen natives to the Roman Catholic faith. Cartier had been authorized to discover new lands "in order the better to do what is pleasing to God, our Creator and Redeemer, and what may be for the increase of his holy and sacred name, and of our holy mother, the Church." (*Jesuit Relations*, vol. i, p. 5.) The letters-patent of the king, October 17, 1540, emphasized that one of the chief objects was to convert the natives and to propagate Christianity in North America. (Rochemonteix, *Les Jésuites et la Nouvelle-France*, Paris, 1895, vol. i, p. 3.) The charter of Henry IV, granting a monopoly of the fur trade to De Monts, stated that [the king was] "moved more especially by a singular zeal and by a pious and steadfast resolution which we have taken, with the aid and assistance of God, . . . to bring about the conversion to Christianity of the tribes inhabiting this country, . . . and to lead and instruct them in the belief and profession of our faith and religion." (Lescarbot, *History of New France*, Champlain Society, vol. ii, pp. 211-212.) His commission from the Lord High Admiral Charles de Montmorency required that "he seek to lead the natives thereof to the profession of the Christian faith, to civilization of manners, an ordered life. . . ." (*Ibid.*, p. 217.)

De Monts apparently accepted with some seriousness the responsibility of converting the natives, for he wrote to the Pope for his blessing. "Inasmuch as his chief object is to establish the Christian religion in the land which his Majesty had been pleased to grant to him and to lead to that faith the poor savage folk . . . he thought fit to ask the blessing of the Pope . . . by a formal letter." (*Ibid.*, pp. 368-369.)

Champlain attributed much of his zeal as an explorer to the opportunity it gave for evangelization, for by it the poor natives were to be led to a knowledge of God. (*Champlain's Voyages*, vol. iii, pp. 43, 91-92, 99 *et seq.*; *cf.* Lescarbot, *op. cit.*, vol. i, pp. 13-14.) "To this end [says Champlain] I exerted myself to find some good friars with zeal and affection for the glory of God that I might persuade them to send some one or to go themselves with me to these countries, and to try to plant there the faith, or at least to do what was possible according to their calling, and thus to observe and ascertain whether any good fruit

The *Récollets,*[1] although only ten years in the country prior to their overthrow by the Jesuits, laid a splendid foundation for successful missionary activity among the Indians. The power of the *Récollets* in this early period, however, was brief and left no lasting mark on the system of ecclesiastical control in Quebec. The rise of that control more properly dates from the coming of the Jesuits in 1625. The Jesuits soon after their arrival were able to usurp the place so worthily held by the *Rêcollets,* both by securing the moral and financial support of the Company of One Hundred Associates,[2] and by bringing pressure to bear in France to prevent the further emigration of *Récollets* to Canada.[3] This accomplished, they began to tighten their hold upon the state, until by the middle of the seventeenth century, Quebec was little more than a Jesuit mission.[4]

This rise of ecclesiastical control was further accelerated

could be gathered there." (*Champlain's Voyages*, vol. iii, p. 101.) Lescarbot's appeal on behalf of Christian missions among the Indians is worthy of the twentieth century. His ground for support is "to chase their ignorance from them, to open unto them the way of salvation and to cause to be known the goodly things, alike natural and supernatural. . . ." (Lescarbot, *op. cit.*, vol. i, p. 11.)

[1] Champlain at first had considerable difficulty in securing support for his mission on the St. Lawrence. It was not until he had enlisted the interest of Houel, the secretary of the king, who "was a man of deep piety and great zeal and love for the honor of God and the extension of religion," he met with success. At Houel's suggestion the *Récollets* were asked to undertake the mission, and after securing sufficient funds in 1615 the five *Récollets,* Fathers Denis, Jamay, d'Albeau le Caron, and a lay-brother, Pacifique de Plessis, founded the first mission in Quebec. (*Champlain's Voyages*, vol. iii, pp. 102-106; *cf.* Kingsford, vol. i, p. 48.)

[2] Eastman, *op. cit.*, p. 15.

[3] Kingsford, *op. cit.*, vol. i, p. 122 *et seq.;* Eastman, pp. 15-16.

[4] "More and more the powers spiritual engrossed the colony. As nearly as might be, the sword was in priestly hands. The Jesuits were all in all." (Parkman, *op. cit.*, p. 245; *cf.* pp. 250-252; Eastman, pp. 16-19.)

by the policy of securing the appointment of government officials for the colony who were highly acceptable to the Society of Jesus. Some even owed official allegiance to the church. Both Montmagny, the governor and successor to Champlain, and De Lisle, his lieutenant, were chevaliers of the Order of Malta.[1] Le Jeune wrote that they,

have given us as governor one of his chevaliers whom I would willingly call, with due respect to all those brave soldiers of Jesus Christ, the honor of Malta and the good fortune of our colony. Monsieur his Lieutenant, who wears this same honorable cross, walks so strictly in his footsteps, that we all have reasons to acknowledge our great obligation to this holy soldiery, constantly armed for the glory of the Christian name.[2]

When it is remembered that the Council was composed of only three members, one of whom was of the character just described, and the second the superior of the Jesuits,[3] at once the theocratic form of this body becomes patent.

The introduction of the popular element into the Council in 1648 by the addition of two inhabitants elected by the syndics of Quebec, Montreal, and Three Rivers,[4] had checked somewhat the dominance of the ecclesiastics. This they resented, and in 1663, partly owing to their influence, the Sovereign Council was established. In the new Council, the edict provided that the bishop, or the first ecclesiastic in the country, should share with the governor-general the power of appointing the other members of the Council, who were to comprise five councilors, an attorney-general, and a clerk.[5]

[1] Parkman, *The Jesuits in North America*, vol. i, pp. 241-246.

[2] *Rel.*, vol. xi, p. 49.

[3] Cahall, p. 14.

[4] *Ibid.*, p. 15.

[5] *Ibid.*, p. 22.

The personnel of the first Sovereign Council was completely of Laval's choosing. For, after the clash between the clergy and D'Avaugour, resulting in the latter's recall, Laval had been invited by the king to nominate a successor. This he did, and Suffray de Mésy [1] was appointed governor.[2] Mésy, however, being ignorant of the situation, the king intrusted the blank commissions to Laval,[3] who filled them with the names of men among whom there was "complete union".[4]

The large service which the missionaries were able to render the less permanent government officials as agents of the state among the Indians was another factor in increasing the authority of the church. The French government was not slow to realize the political as well as the religious significance of missions among the Indians. The "black robes'" intimate knowledge of the language, habits and customs of the savages rendered them invaluable as interpreters,[5] and as the medium of communication between the government and the natives.[6] Denonville wrote to Seignelay,

> though the interests of the Gospel should not engage us to keep missionaries in all the Iroquois and other Indian villages, the

[1] Usually spelled Mézy. The spelling given is that of his signature to the minutes of the Sovereign Council.

[2] Charlevoix, *op. cit.*, vol. iii, pp. 73-74; Eastman, *op. cit.*, p. 48.

[3] Eastman, p. 49. Eastman's interpretation here may be open to doubt. The document states that five persons were to be appointed whose "*expeditions*" have been delivered to the bishop. (*C. A.*, B. 1, p. 109.)

[4] *Lettres de la Vénérable Mère Marie de l'Incarnation*, p. 589, cited by Eastman, p. 50.

[5] Charlevoix, *op. cit.*, vol. iii, p. 151; *ibid.*, vol. v, pp. 149-150.

[6] *Ibid.*, vol. iii, pp. 267-269, 302-303; vol. v, p. 236; *Colon. Docs. N. Y.*, vol. ix, pp. 297, 713.

interest of civil government for the advantage of trade must induce us so to manage as always to have some there; for these Indian tribes can never govern themselves except by those missionaries, who alone are able to maintain them in our interests and to prevent their revolting against us every day.[1]

The missionaries, and more especially the Jesuits, not only were most familiar with Indian affairs,[2] but they were able to obtain the secret information [3] which so often enabled French diplomacy to retain the friendship of the Indians and to outwit their English rivals.

It was through their services in negotiating treaties, more especially with the Indians, that the missionaries were able to make, perhaps, their largest contribution to the state.[4] Some of these, such as Father John de Lamberville,[5] and Father Bruyas,[6] seem to have become expert in diplomacy. Such service, in a time when the very life of the colony was threatened by Indian wars, was bound to be recognized, and to win prestige and authority for the clergy as a whole.

It is doubtful, however, whether the clergy would have

[1] *Colon. Docs. N. Y.*, vol. ix, p. 440; *cf.* Eastman, *op. cit.*, p. 255.

[2] Charlevoix, *op. cit.*, vol. iii, p. 268; Eastman, p. 210; *Colon. Docs. N. Y.*, vol. ix, p. 440.

[3] "It was not that the nation was better disposed to embrace Christianity; but it was not useless to religion, and it was important to the colony to have among these savages persons invested with a character capable of impressing them, whose presence assured them of a desire to live in peace with them; who could enlighten their conduct, notify the governor-general of all their proceedings, gain them by affability, or at least make friends among them—above all, discover and disconcert the intrigues of the English. . . ." (Charlevoix, vol. v, p. 155; *cf. ibid.*, vol. iv, p. 239; vol. v, pp. 153, 203.)

[4] The governor-general cannot be without the service of the Jesuits in making treaties with the governors of New England and New York, as well as with the Iroquois." (La Hontan, *op. cit.*, p. 365; *cf.* Eastman, p. 23.)

[5] Charlevoix, *op. cit.*, vol. iii, pp. 220, 253, 267, 299.

[6] *Ibid.*, vol. v, pp. 107, 140.

been able to continue their influence, or whether the church, as a whole, would have been able to maintain its control to the extent that it did under the ambitious colonial policy of Colbert, had it not been for the arrival, in 1759, of Vicar-general Laval.

Laval undoubtedly made the largest contribution to ecclesiastical control in Quebec ever made by any single ecclesiastic. This he accomplished, both by having the church become directly dependent upon the Papal See, and by giving unity to the ecclesiastical forces. Strongly ultramontane, his consecration by the pope as vicar-general, thus evading the king's nomination, and his victory over the Vicar-General Queylus, the appointee of the Archbishop of Rouen, was a triumph for the papacy and a defeat for the Gallican church.

At this time there were two great parties among the Roman Catholics of France: the Gallican or National party, and the Ultramontane or Papal party. The first held that the temporal sword belonged to the king, and the spiritual power to the church in the kingdom;[1] while the second maintained the pope to be Christ's vicegerent, supreme over earthly rulers, as well as exercising jurisdiction over all the clergy of Christendom.[2] The chief exponents of this Ultramontane or Papal party were the Jesuits,[3] so that it is not difficult to understand Laval's intolerant attitude in New France towards the struggle for temporary supremacy

[1] Champeaux, *Recueil général du droit civil écclésiastique français*, 2d ed., vol. i, p. 199 *et seq.; cf. Cambridge Modern History*, vol. ii, p. 95; vol. v, pp. 72-77.

[2] Parkman, *Old Régime*, p. 95; also "Gallicanism," *The Catholic Encyclopedia*, vol. vi, p. 354.

[3] Wilhelm Moeller, *History of the Christian Church*, Reformation, pp. 262-265. For a time the Jesuits did take the side of Louis XIV (R. Travers Smith, *The Church in France*, p. 378).

carried on by Frontenac, or towards the episcopal claims of Queylus.[1]

During the years 1655, 1656 and 1657, just previous to the departure of Laval for Canada, the French clergy had been remonstrating against the abuses to which they considered themselves subject. So effective was their agitation that the king, in March, 1666, issued a declaration containing thirty articles, upholding the clergy in their immunities, franchises, liberties, rights and prerogatives.[2] It is clear that Laval was determined to secure these for the church in New France, and from the very beginning laid his plans accordingly.

Louis XIV assumed charge of the government in 1661. The king, although only twenty-three years old, had welcomed the theory of absolute monarchy founded on divine right. "In his eyes royalty was a divine institution: sovereigns were the representatives of God upon the earth, and on this account participated in his power and infallibility."[3] The Sorbonne further supported this theory by declaring, in 1663, that it admitted no authority of the pope over the king's temporal dominion, nor his superiority to a general council, nor infallibility apart from the church's consent. A practical expression was soon given to this claim by the attempt of the king, in 1673, to extend the right of *régale*[4] to all the churches. This brought him into conflict with Pope Innocent XI.[5] In order to put an end to this contro-

[1] Parkman, *Old Régime*, p. 97 *et seq.*

[2] Champeaux, *op. cit.*, vol. i, p. 181 *et seq.*

[3] Duruy's *Hist. of France*, p. 417.

[4] The right of receiving the revenues of vacant sees, and of conferring such sees.

[5] *Cambridge Modern History*, vol. v, pp. 52, 85; *cf.* also *Cath. Ency.*, vol. vi, p. 354.

versy, Louis XIV called an assembly of the French clergy, who, in the declaration of March, 1682, upheld the authority of the king and the autonomy of the church in four propositions, which may be summarized as follows:

1. God has not given to St. Peter and his successors any power, either direct or indirect, over temporal matters; therefore in these matters the pope has no jurisdiction over the king or his subjects.
2. The Gallican church approves the decrees of the Council of Constance declaring œcumenical councils superior to the pope in spiritual matters, and holds them as still in full force.[1]
3. The usages and rules of the Gallican church in the kingdom, shall remain unchanged, and it is to the glory of the Holy See that they should so remain.
4. The decisions of the pope in questions of faith are not final until ratified by the church.[2]

Laval took good care that this victory for the king and the Gallican church in France should not be repeated in Canada. Indeed, his consecration by the pope as vicar-apostolic, thus evading the king's nomination, had been a triumph for the papacy. The anger of the Gallicans, and the opposition of the Archbishop of Rouen, as well as the protests of the parliaments of Rouen and Paris, at this exclusion of Canada from the Concordat, had been all to no

[1] The fourth and fifth sessions of the council of Constance declared that the council represented the church, and that every person, no matter of what dignity—even the pope—was bound to obey it in what concerned the extirpation of schism and the reform of the church; that even the pope, if he resisted obstinately, might be constrained by process of law to obey it in the above-mentioned points. (*Cath. Ency.*, vol. vi, p. 354; *cf.* Smith. *op. cit.*, p. 234.)

[2] *Déclaration du clergé de France sur la puissance ecclésiastique*, Champeaux, *op. cit.*, vol. i, p. 198; *cf. Cambridge Modern History*, vol. v, pp. 85-86.

purpose.[1] The decline of the influence of the Gallican church in directing ecclesiastical affairs in Canada, was brought about still further, as has been pointed out, by Laval's successful attempt, on his arrival in Canada, to oust the Sulpician Vicar-general, Queylus, appointee of the Archbishop of Rouen. This determination of Laval to uphold the papacy at the expense of the Gallican church,[2] and the success which attended it, won for the papacy a hold upon Quebec which it still possesses.

Laval, no doubt, recognized, in accepting the appointment of vicar-apostolic, that he would be made Bishop of Quebec. As early as 1647, in constituting the Upper Council, the king had made provision that the council should be composed "of the Governor of Quebec, the Governor of Montreal, and the Superior of the Jesuits until there should be a bishop."[3] In 1662, Laval received from Louis XIV the assurance that he would petition the pope for the erection of a see of Quebec, which he did two years later. The king also assigned for the proposed bishopric the revenues of the abbey of Maubec.[4]

[1] Parkman, *Old Régime* (1874), pp. 96-97; *cf. ibid.*, Champlain Edition, vol. i, pp. 152-155.

[2] *C. A.*, M. 128, p. 389.

[3] Brumath, *Bishop Laval*, Makers of Canada, vol. ii, p. 25.

[4] "The choice made by your Holiness of the person of the Sieur de Laval, Bishop of Petraea, to go in the capacity of apostolic vicar to exercise episcopal functions in Canada has been attended by many advantages to this growing church. We have reason to expect still greater results if it please your Holiness to permit him to continue there the same functions in the capacity of bishop of the place, by establishing for this purpose an episcopal see in Quebec; and we hope that your Holiness will be the more inclined to this since we have already provided for the maintenance of the bishop and his canons by consenting to the perpetual union of the abbey of Maubec with the future bishopric. This is why we beg you to grant to the Bishop of Petraea the title of Bishop of Quebec upon our nomination and prayer, with power to exercise in this capacity the episcopal functions in all Canada." (*Mandements*, vol. i, p. 82 *et seq.; cf. ibid.*, pp. 131-132.)

To Laval the bishop's see represented increased power, and he left no stone unturned to secure it. He acknowledges this to the Propaganda:

I have never till now sought the episcopacy, . . . I have, however, learned by long experience how unguarded is the position of an apostolic vicar against those who are entrusted with political affairs, I mean the officers of the court, perpetual rivals and despisers of the ecclesiastical power, who have nothing more common to object than that the authority of the apostolic vicar is doubtful and should be restricted within certain limits. This is why, after having maturely considered everything, I have resolved to resign this function and to return no more to New France unless a see be erected there, and unless I be provided and furnished with bulls constituting me its occupant. Such is the purpose of my journey to France and the object of my desires.[1]

The influence of Gallicanism was too strong in France, however, and the king insisted that the new diocese should be dependent upon the Metropolitan of Rouen, while the Propaganda refused to establish it unless "as an immediate dependency of the Holy See."[2] This conflict delayed the papal bull for the erection of the bishopric. From a letter of Laval to the Propaganda in September, 1669, the difficulty seems to have been clear to him, for he says:

I know well how much I owe to your Eminences who confer upon me all sorts of benefits; and, as I have heard, it is not owing to you that the chief business of this church, namely, the exaltation thereof to the rank of the Episcopate, has failed of accomplishment. It is said that the delay arises from the protest of the Archbishop of Rothoma [Rouen], who maintains that the Episcopate in Canada should be subject to his

[1] Brumath, *op. cit.*, vol. ii, pp. 130-131.

[2] *Ibid.*, pp. 132-133.

Archbishopric. And, assuredly, if there is nothing more involved, and your Eminences judge that this ought to be done, I willingly agree thereto; and, lest any damage be caused to the order and liberty of the church, it would be expedient perhaps that this arrangement should be made only for a time—as long, that is to say, as he is so bishop, and that it is not yet fitting that an archbishop should be appointed, inasmuch as once such appointment was made, that subjection would cease. Concerning these matters I have written something to His Holiness, as also, shortly, concerning other matters that pertain to our affairs.[1]

This letter shows that Laval, in his eagerness to obtain the episcopate in Canada, was willing to have it continue under the Archbishopric of Rouen during the archbishop's incumbency. He insisted, however, that "Nothing stable is to be hoped for until something definite be determined concerning the fixity of the episcopate and of the parishes."[1] In the meantime he requested that the papal authority be maintained by the appointment of a parish priest direct from Rome.[2]

Five years later, on the first of October, 1674, the importunity of Laval was rewarded, for the Papal Court issued the bull establishing the Archbishopric of Quebec. This was made possible by an understanding having been reached between Louis XIV and Pope Clement X, through which the right of nomination became the prerogative of the king, and the bishopric became directly dependent upon

[1] Laval to their Eminences, Sept. 30, 1669, *C. A.*, M. 128, p. 389.

[2] "If the matter of the Episcopate cannot be settled this year, and the titles of the Parishes, which are so necessary, cannot be obtained, your Eminences will do what is essential and most effective in supporting the Christian Faith, if, at least by the Apostolic Authority, a Parish Priest be appointed as soon as possible in the church of Quebec." (*Ibid.*)

the See of Rome.[1] The king's right of nomination was conceded on the ostensible ground that it was in return for the assignation of the abbey of Maubec.[2] The bishop was to have the full episcopal rights and benefits of the new see, together with the cure of souls in the suppressed parochial church.[3] Sufficient canonries and prebends were to be established to constitute the officers and holders of these a chapter.[4]

This increased episcopal authority came at an opportune time to meet the growing power of the state. The theo-

[1] "And we do grant to the same King Louis and his successors, in consideration of the assignation, made as above with the consent of the said King Louis, to the aforesaid Episcopal Board, of the aforesaid Abbey, the right of nomination to the aforesaid Church of Quebec, in case the same shall be temporarily deprived, through resignation or death, or in any other manner, of the consoling ministry of a pastor; and to him who, or to those who found and endow canonries and prebends and other ecclesiastical benefices and ministries from their own goods, always, be it understood, in accord with the will of the Bishop—we [in similar case] grant the right of patronage; but such nomination [to permanent office], as far as the Church of Quebec is concerned, [shall belong] to us, or to our successor, the Roman Pontiff as the time in which canonries, prebends and benefices and ministries of the like nature fall vacant for presentation, and when such appointments are due to be made in presence of the Ordinary of Quebec [Bishop in office]. (Bull, Establishing the Archbishopric of Quebec, Oct. 1st, 1674, *Mandements,* vol. i, p. 82 *et seq.*)

[2] *Ibid.*

[3] "This Parochial Church, the title and description of Parochial Church being suppressed and extinguished for all time, we do erect and form into a Cathedral Church, directly subject unto the Apostolic See, with the appointment to the said church of Quebec of a Bishop who shall preside over the same with full episcopal rights and dignity, and shall discharge in the same and in its diocese all and sundry those matters, to be enumerated below, that belong to the jurisdiction and dignity of the episcopal order and the exercise of the pastorate, and that bear upon and pertain to the summoning and holding session of the diocesan synod." (Bull, Establishing the Archbishopric of Quebec, Oct. 1, 1674, *Mandements*, vol. i, p. 82 *et seq.*)

[4] *Ibid.*

cratic cabal said to have been chosen by Laval, after his return to Canada in 1663,[1] had been shortlived; for as soon as Mésy knew he had the support of Colbert,[2] he broke with the bishop, and openly defied the clerical party.[3] His successors, Tracy, Courcelle, and Talon, were even more successful in undermining the temporal influence of the clerical forces.[4]

Thus, before the arrival of Frontenac (in 1672), who still further weakened the authority of the church,[5] the zenith of ecclesiastical control under the French régime had been reached. The ambitious policy of Colbert had given a new strength and dignity to temporal affairs, both at home and abroad.[6] New France, under the able administration of Talon, had begun to be developed. The fur-company mission-station was giving place to the well-organized colony. Peace was no longer to be preserved between the governor and clergy, by the submission of the state to the spiritual and temporal control of the church.[7]

Only for a brief period under the administration of Denonville (1685-1689) did the church ever regain, under the French régime, even the semblance of her former power.[8] This revival in the temporal authority of the hier-

[1] Eastman, *op. cit.*, p. 49.

[2] Colbert held that it was of vital importance "to hold in a just balance" the temporal authority of the king and his ministers and the spiritual authority of the bishop and the Jesuits, "in such a manner, nevertheless, that the latter shall be inferior to the former." (*Ibid.*, p. 99.)

[3] *Ibid.*, pp. 79-89.

[4] *Ibid.*, p. 90 *et seq.*

[5] *Ibid.*, p. 263.

[6] Duruy's *History of France*, p. 423 *et seq.*

[7] Parkman, *Old Régime* (1874), pp. 106-107.

[8] Eastman, *op. cit.*, p. 260.

archy, far from showing any permanent tendency, rather represented a reaction following the anti-clericalism of Frontenac. It is true that the king urged Denonville to preserve harmonious relations with the bishop; he was to do his utmost for the cause of religion, and was to be careful not to exceed his own authority, or to encroach upon that of the bishop.[1]

After the failure of Denonville's Indian policy, and the return of Frontenac, the temporal authority of the church again declined.[2] In theory, the church remained as ultramontane as formerly; in practice, more and more the Gallican influence was felt.

Although Laval had succeeded in making the Archbishopric of Quebec dependent upon the See of Rome, the decline in the actual power of the church which followed the

[1] "He knows that the chief and essential duty is to satisfy the requirements of religion, upon which depends the blessing which may be looked for from Heaven, and without which nothing can have a happy issue, and His Majesty desires that the authority entrusted to the said M. de Denonville should be employed chiefly to promote, as far as lies in his power, the glory of God throughout the colony, and the spread of the Christian Religion, as far as this can be done among the neighboring Indians.

"To this intent His Majesty desires that he may, in all things, preserve harmonious relations with the Abbé de Chevrières, appointed to the Bishopric of Quebec; that he lend [the Abbé] every assistance and protection in whatsoever pertains to his functions, and that he contribute by his attention and diligence to all that may concern the spiritual welfare of the Colony, without, nevertheless, in any way exceeding his functions in that respect, or doing anything on his own authority, or without the participation of the said Bishop; and it will be the easier to coöperate with him for the spiritual welfare of the Colony inasmuch as the said Bishop, being a man of exemplary piety, will have no difficulty in acting in concert with a Governor whom he finds favorably disposed to all that concerns spiritual things." (Instructions to Denonville, March 10, 1685, *C. A.*, B. 11, p. 150; *cf. C. A.*, B, vol. xvi, pt. i, p. 133 *et seq.*)

[2] Eastman, *op. cit.*, pp. 263-265.

struggle between Laval and Frontenac and which accompanied the rise of Gallican influence paved the way for definite pressure by the state for the purpose of further limiting ecclesiastical control. This pressure evinced itself in resistance to the hierarchy in Sovereign Council, in the matter of tithes, in restrictions upon religious houses, in restrictions upon the public ministry of the church and in various matters involving the relation of the church and parishioners. The theory used in developing this pressure was that the king was the head of the church. When pressure began to be exerted with a strong hand the state easily overthrew the power of the hierarchy in the Sovereign Council, and thwarted the repeated attempts of the clergy to have the tithes increased and to regulate their collection. The erection of religious houses and their regulation were handled with equal efficiency. In the public ministry of the church, such matters as the number of candidates to be allowed to study for the church, the use of the pulpit as an agency of publicity, as well as the attitude toward the brandy trade, reveal the strong hand which the state held over the church. Questions of church polity, such as the protection of the rights of parishioners, curé and seignior against encroachment on the part of the bishop, which to-day would be entirely within the ecclesiastical jurisdiction of the church, were actively dealt with by the state.

In the Sovereign Council, as has been mentioned, the bishop soon lost his place of great influence and power. Instead of continuing to select its members, he became only an honorary member himself. In 1703 his right to be represented by an ecclesiastic was abolished, and a clerical councilor was appointed to be the permanent representative of the church interests.[1] After 1668, Cahall says he ceased

[1] Cahall, *op. cit.*, p. 151.

to exercise his right to sign the minutes,[1] which, seven years later, became the duty of the *Intendant*. Evidence is lacking even to show that he ever voted in the Council. His influence was rather exerted indirectly through friends of the hierarchy in the council.[2] At times, however, his regular attendance at the meetings of the Council, and his interest in the deliberations, occasioned some uneasiness. The minister complained to Duchesneau, in 1677, that, as the bishop was assuming too independent an authority, it would perhaps be better that he should not have a seat in the council.[3]

The same attitude was shown toward the aggression of the church in the matter of tithes. From the first, the colonists appear to have opposed tithes, looking upon them as most burdensome. Laval's request, in 1667, that the tithes be established and collected, brought such a storm of protest from the inhabitants that the Sovereign Council reduced the tithes to one twenty-sixth, and exempted new land from tithes for the first five years.[4] Naturally, the reduction of the tithes met with strong opposition from the clergy. With the growth of the colony, new parishes had to be formed in sparsely-settled districts, where the income from the reduced tithes was insufficient to support the curé. The clergy sought to have the tithes restored to one-thirteenth. Pressure was brought to bear in France.[5] In a

[1] Cahall, *op. cit.*, p. 151. Cahall seems to have been mistaken in this, for there are numerous cases of Bishop Laval's signature affixed to the minutes as late as October, 1670. *Jugements et Dél.*, vol. i, pp. 575, 613, 617, 637 and 638.

[2] Cahall, p. 151.

[3] *Ibid.*, p. 153.

[4] Charlevoix, *op. cit.*, vol. iii, p. 24; *cf.* Eastman, *op. cit.*, p. 106.

[5] "These representations and clamors only ceased when the superior council had reduced the tithes to a twenty-sixth." (Brasseur, *Histoire du Canada, de son église et de ses missions*, p. 112; *cf.* Charlevoix, vol. iii, pp. 24-25.)

letter to Frontenac, dated June 7, 1689, the king states that he will inquire whether it is possible to increase the tithes again to one-thirteenth without placing too heavy a burden upon the settlers.[1] The king, however, must have deemed it unwise to make any change, for nothing was done, and, in an edict of 1679, the regulation of 1667 with regard to tithes, was upheld.[2] It was further stated that, "in case the income from the lease is not sufficient for the support of the curé, the necessary augmentation shall be fixed by our Council at Quebec, and shall be furnished by both the seignior of the fief and the inhabitants thereof."[3]

The attempt of Bishop Saint-Valier and the Governor, La Barre, to enforce the edict, on the basis of a minimum stipend of 500 *livres* for each curé, was objected to by the king in 1684 in a letter to the bishop, on the ground that the stipend was too high, considering the poverty of the people, and that it was opposed to the interests of the colony.[4]

The clergy not only refused to accept the regulations of 1667, 1679, and 1680, as final, but some of their number claimed from their parishioners tithes on all the products, from both cultivated and uncultivated land and even from the stock. To meet the situation, the Sovereign Council passed an ordinance in 1705, that the tithes were to remain at one twenty-sixth of the grain only, to be delivered at the presbytery; and further, that the curés were forbidden to make any regulations whatsoever regarding the tithes.[5] In

[1] *C. A.*, B. 15, p. 273 *et seq.; cf.* also *Colon. Docs. N. Y.*, vol. iii, pp. 151-152.

[2] "The tithes shall be levied according to the regulations of the Fourth of September, One Thousand Six Hundred and Sixty Seven." *Edits et Ord.* (1803), vol. i, art. ii, p. 244.

[3] *Ibid.*, art. iv.

[4] Charlevoix, *op. cit.*, vol. iii, p. 25; *cf. Colon. Docs. N. Y.*, vol. ix, pp. 150-151.

[5] *Edits et Ord.* (1854), p. 308.

the following year, the Sovereign Council passed another ordinance, forbidding the curés to ask for tithes, or the inhabitants to pay them, except in the manner laid down by His Majesty.[1] These two decisions of the Sovereign Council were so unpopular with the clergy that, in 1707, they appealed to the King in Council. The King, however, upheld the decisions of the Sovereign Council[2] of November 18, 1705, and February 1, 1706, and forbade the clergy to make any innovations in the matter of tithes, under pain of a heavy fine.[3]

Twenty-five years later, in 1732, the curés renewed their petition to have the tithes augmented, on the plea that "three-fourths of the curés have not enough to live on." The court was even less sympathetic. In a letter, the minister, Maurepas, wrote as follows:

The King has not judged proper to augment to the thirteenth minot, the tithes of the curés. Out of sixty-two curés, twenty-seven have a revenue of from eight hundred to two thousand four hundred *livres*, and thirty-five of from one hundred and ninety to seven hundred and thirty, outside of their perquisites, which is amply sufficient for them to live on. . . . .

His Majesty has not thought fit to make any changes in the Canadian usage regarding tithes, and it is useless to insist on it any further. He knows that, in spite of any diminutions that may have taken place, the livings are good, and far from thinking of increasing the supplements already given, he may eventually decrease them, if he learns that the curés, for interested motives, have sought to turn the inhabitants from commerce or cultivation beneficial to the colony.[4]

[1] *Jugements et Dél.*, vol. v, pp. 230-231.

[2] *Edits et Ord.* (1854), p. 311.

[3] *Ibid.*, p. 310.

[4] Letter of M. de Maurepas to Beauharnois and Hocquart, April 1, 1732, *C. A.*, B. 57, pt. i, p. 49.

The opposition, both of the court and the people, against increasing the tithes, was equally pronounced against the use of undue influence in collecting them. In some of the country parishes, the bishops had excommunicated those who had neglected to pay the tithes. This rigorous action did not long go unchallenged. Complaints soon reached the court, whose attitude is seen in the following letter:

I have spoken to the Lord Bishop of Quebec on the disadvantages which you point out to me as resulting from the execution of the order, given by him, to refuse absolution and the Paschal Communion to those inhabitants of the country districts who have not paid their tithes; [and] I have notified him that it was the desire of His Majesty that he should take other measures to secure this end, and it is desirable to have information as to the expedient you propose to adopt.[1]

Other and milder expedients were used, but there seems to have been no improvement, on the part of the people, in meeting their material obligations to the church. A dispatch from Beauharnois and Hocquart, in 1731, states that a large number of the inhabitants still neglected to pay the tithes, or paid them only in part. Regret was expressed, as this was alike prejudicial to the consciences of the people and to good order in the state. The curés were held to be to some extent responsible, and it was pointed out that much of the difficulty might be avoided, if the curés were more prompt in collecting the tithes.[2] In still another dispatch of the same year, they wrote, "We have proposed to His Lordship the Bishop to issue a pastoral letter (*mandement*) instructing the people of the imperative obligation which they are under to pay the tithes to their curés."[3]

[1] *C. A.*, B. 23, pt. ii, p. 279.

[2] *C. A.*, C^{11}, vol. 107, p. 198.

[3] Corresp. Gen., vol. liv, cited by Gosselin, *L'Eglise du Canada*, p. 150.

These two dispatches disclose the policy of the government toward the church in the latter period of French rule; the tithes were to be collected in such a way, and at such a time, as was likely to cause the least prejudice among the people; moral suasion was to be substituted for compulsion.

Religious houses and religious communities, also, came under the careful scrutiny of the king. No foundation or new establishment was permitted in New France, unless it had the formal consent of the king, and all bequests to such as contravened this regulation were invalid.[1]

In 1700, before the passing of the above edict, the king had repeatedly refused to grant letters patent, even after the establishment had been made by the authority of the bishop.[2] With regard to the Ursulines at Three Rivers, the bishop was to assume responsibility for the members,

[1] " Art. 1. It is our pleasure, in accordance with the commands given and regulations made for the interior of our kingdom, that no foundation or new establishment of houses and religious communities, hospitals, refuges, congregations, confraternities, colleges, or other religious or lay bodies or communities, be made in our colony of America: save by virtue of our express permission given by our letters patent, registered in our Superior Council of the said colonies in the form that will be prescribed hereinafter.

" Art. 2. We forbid the making of any disposition by last will or testament for the foundation of any new establishment of the nature of those mentioned in the preceding article, or in favor of persons who may be intrusted with the foundation of such establishments: the whole under pain of nullity; which requirement shall be observed, even if the will or testament has been made under condition of obtaining our letters-patent." (*Edits et Ord.* (1854), vol. i, pp. 576-577; *cf.* Charlevoix, *op. cit.*, vol. iii, p. 28.)

[2] " I wrote to you last year that His Majesty had been pleased to allow this establishment to remain since you had founded it, but that he was not willing to give it His approval. He instructs me to inform you that He will not grant the letters-patent for which you apply." (The Minister to the Bishop of Quebec, May 5, 1700, *C. A.*, Moreau St. Méry, F[3], vol. vi, p. 78 *et seq.*)

should they become dependent;[1] and the king further reminded him to improve the old establishments rather than to found new ones.[2]

The encroachment of the bishop on the rights of religious orders or secular institutions was closely watched. The minister wrote to the bishop that,

His Majesty has also learned that you have authoritatively removed the Nursing Sisters (*religieuses hospitallières*) from the *Hotel-Dieu*, to put them in charge of the General Hospital. His Majesty will have this disapproved of, and has commanded me to write to you that He desires you to send these religious sisters back to the Hotel-Dieu, as it is not His intention to make a convent of this hospital. He wishes that it should be governed by administrators like all the other general hospitals in the kingdom. He instructs me to give His orders accordingly to the said Srs. de Callères and de Champigney. I am now writing to them at the same time to act in concert with you in this matter, and to leave to you the care of removing these religious persons in whatever manner you think fit—His Majesty being pleased to intrust you with this duty, as long as it be performed.[3]

[1] "His Majesty . . . has read with sincere sorrow reports which have been sent him from many places, of the evil effects which follow your founding religious houses for men and women, and he has been assured that already it is possible to see to what suffering the Ursuline Nuns, established by you at Three Rivers, are certain to be exposed; and without taking account of this, you have caused them to admit new members who are without dowry. Be good enough to make provision for the future of these young women, in case that, through lack of funds, it should be found necessary to dissolve this community." (*Ibid.*)

[2] "He commands me, furthermore, to inform you that you will please him much if you will make every effort to improve the old establishments of the communities of nuns, which are now only too numerous, instead of founding new ones, which cannot be suitable to a colony like that of Canada." (*Ibid.*)

[3] *C. A.*, F[3], vol. vi, p. 78 *et seq.*

The public ministry of the church had to conform to public policy. While the parish priests were to apply themselves, principally, to the education of youth, the bishop was to see that the instruction was not of such a character as to induce too many of the young people to train for religious orders.[1]

The state demanded the right, notwithstanding the opposition of the bishop and clergy, of having all proclamations and other official announcements published from the parish pulpits; and further, that proper titles be given the officials mentioned in these documents.[2]

In the matter of the attitude and influence of the clergy on public questions, the state assumed the right even to dictate the policy of the church. The praiseworthy stand taken by the clergy against the brandy trade had aroused strong opposition from the officials, the *habitants,* and more especially the traders, who alleged that the traffic was necessary to the economic prosperity of the colony. It is evident that the minister shared this view, and determined that the clergy must cease their opposition to the brandy trade, for he wrote to Saint-Valier that,

The continued complaints of those who are trading in Canada,

[1] "Above all, be very careful to establish in all the parishes none but good, capable priests who will apply themselves principally to the education of youth, taking care at the same time not to carry too far instructions tending towards the ecclesiastical estate, as it is of importance that there should be admitted to it only those who are necessary for the good of the colony." (The Minister to the Abbé de Chevrières, May 31, 1686, *C. A.*, B. 12, p. 83.)

[2] "His Majesty desires that you give the necessary orders to have the ordinances of the Governor-General and the *Intendant* published from the pulpit in the same way as these ordinances are usually published in the kingdom, this being necessary to the advantage of His Majesty's service; it is his will that in doing so the title of '*Monseigneur*' be given to the Governor-General, but not to the *Intendant*. . . ." (*C. A.*, B. 12, p. 84; *cf.* Eastman, *op. cit.*, p. 107.)

and of the greater part of the Colonists, oblige me to address to you the same remonstrances as the late Marquis de Seignelay sent to you last year, regarding the obstacles which are put in the way of the traffic in brandy and wine, in which they meet interference through immoderate zeal on the part of some of the clergy, under the pretext that the Indians are making an abuse of these things. And as it has appeared to me that the King has previously guarded against this by his ordinance of the 24th of May, 1679, it is of great importance that you should take the trouble to inquire very carefully into what is being done by the clergy in this and other matters, which may needlessly disturb the consciences of the people, so that, by your prudence, you may restrict them to the bounds within which they should confine themselves in their ministrations. It would even be well that you should see to it their zeal is not caused by personal passions and interests. Indeed, I cannot help repeating what was written to you last year in this respect, namely, that the subjects of the King could not carry on in Canada any trade so useful to the kingdom as that in wine and brandy, and that in none have they so great an advantage over the English and Dutch. Moreover, it seems to me that nowhere in the Christian world has a case of conscience been made of the sale of brandy, the use of which in itself is very beneficial; and that the French were established in Canada nearly a century before it occurred to anyone to raise this question, which it would seem that we might properly confine to the prevention of the abuse of these things, as far as possible, as is the custom elsewhere.[1]

The policy of the church likewise came under the exacting regulation of the king, who "as protector of the holy canons" held himself obliged "to look to it well that the discipline of the church is observed even in the most distant countries under our authority."[2] It is true that the

[1] The minister to Saint-Valier, April 7, 1691, *C. A.*, B. 16, pt. i, p. 134; *cf.* Eastman, *op. cit.*, pp. 26, 72-82, 197-200, 222-227, 243, 275-292.

[2] *Edits et Ord.* (1803), vol. i, p. 243.

Sovereign Council never had the courage to attack the bishop directly;[1] but the correspondence of the ministers shows plainly that the king and his ministers had no such scruples.

In all the relations of the bishop, whether with the Papal See or the people, the king was actively supreme. On the question of receiving bulls from Rome, the bishop was plainly told by the minister that,

His Majesty has not thought fit, as yet, to permit you to take Bulls, the affairs of Rome not being in such a state that he can give a like permission to the other priests who are nominated to bishoprics; but His Majesty trusts to you to come here whenever you think proper, being persuaded that you will do nothing in this but what you think most advantageous for his service.[2]

The king likewise held a firm hand over the ecclesiastical court. Several times the Sovereign Council reversed its decisions.[3] Important cases were taken to France, as is seen in the decree of the king regarding the claims of the Bishop of Quebec, the Seminary, and the Chapter, in 1692.

The King in Council considering the decision of the eleventh of January, sixteen hundred and ninety-two, made by His Grace the Archbishop of Paris, duke and peer of France, and Father de la Chaize, confessor to His Majesty, with the consent of the Lord Bishop of Quebec and of Father de Brisacier, Superior of the Seminary for Foreign Missions, acting both for the said Seminary and Chapter of Quebec regarding several questions in dispute between the said Bishop and the said Seminary and Chapter, by which decision the said Lord Archbishop and Father de la Chaize have pronounced upon all the points in dispute: His Majesty desiring that the decision have

[1] Cahall, *op. cit.*, p. 153.

[2] *C. A.*, B. 12, p. 83.

[3] Cahall, p. 154.

full and entire execution, His Majesty being in council, hath ordained, and doth ordain that the said decision of the Eleventh of January, Sixteen Hundred and Ninety Two shall be executed according to its form and tenor, to which effect all necessary letters shall be despatched.[1]

The same was true with regard to excommunication. Although it was an acknowledged weapon of the church, the king refused to permit the bishop to use it against the inhabitants of the country districts who did not pay their tithes.[2] Even while Laval did make use of it in the fight against the brandy trade, the firm stand of the governor, and the violent opposition of the inhabitants, led him for a time to revoke his decree of excommunication.[3]

The Sovereign Council, further, attempted to protect the parishioner against defamation of character by a priest, as in the Rolland case. In this case it fined the *habitant* who, at the curé's request, had taken the parishioners' signatures testifying to the questionable character of Rolland;[4] it forbade the ecclesiastics to take any further action,[5] or the clergy to read any documents at the church doors that did not deal with purely ecclesiastical matters, or had not been ordered by the courts.[6]

The parochial clergy, previous to 1679, served their parishes under commission, and were removable at the pleasure of the bishop or the superior of the Seminary of Quebec.[7]

[1] *Edits et Ord.* (1803), vol. i, pp. 274-275.

[2] *C. A.*, B. 23, pt. ii, p. 279; *cf. C. A.*, Moreau St. Méry, F³, vol. vi, p. 78.

[3] Eastman, *op. cit.*, pp. 72, 74-75.

[4] *Jugements et Dél.*, vol. ii, p. 132; *cf. ibid.*, pp. 97-100, 103-105, 108-109.

[5] *Ibid.*, pp. 121-122; *cf.* Eastman, pp. 184-187.

[6] *Ibid.*, p. 132; *cf.* Cahall, *op. cit.*, p. 153.

[7] *Edits et Ord.* (1803), vol. i, p. 243 *et seq.*; Charlevoix, *op. cit.*, vol. iii, p. 22.

This arrangement was considered unsatisfactory by the seigniors and *habitants*. All the tithes had been payable to the Seminary, and the parishioners thought that they had often to pay when they had received little service.[1] Notwithstanding that both the bishop and the *Intendant* Duchesneau favored the old plan, Colbert informed them that removable priests were "directly contrary to the canons of the Councils, and to the laws, ordinances, and usages of the kingdom."[2]

A new edict was passed in 1679 under which the curés were to be settled permanently in the parishes, and were to enjoy the revenue of them, independently of either the bishop or the superior of the seminary.[3]

Some of the immense patronage[4] which the bishop lost

[1] Eastman, *op. cit.*, p. 171.

[2] *Ibid.*, pp. 171, 172.

[3] "The tithes over and above the offerings and dues of the church shall belong entirely to each of the curés throughout the extent of the parish in which he is, and in which he is established permanently, instead of the removable priest, who has hitherto ministered to it. . . . Each curé shall have the choice of collecting the tithes, and using them as he sees fit, or of leasing them to private individuals, residents of the parish, but neither the seigniors of the fief where the church is situated, nor the nobility, nor officers, nor the inhabitants corporally shall have the right to collect them. . . . If, in the course of time, it is necessary to increase the number of parishes owing to the growth in population, the tithes in that portion which shall be separated from the original territory, composing at present a single parish, shall belong entirely to the curé of the new church there established, with the offerings and dues of the said new church, and the curé of the old church shall have no claim to any recognition or compensation." (*Edits et Ord.* (1803), vol. i, p. 243 *et seq.*)

[4] ". . . . and the said bishop shall cause the cure of souls to be exercised in the aforesaid suppressed parochial church on alternate weeks, or as shall otherwise seem best to him through the present rector of the same, with conservation to the said rector of one and all of his emoluments, both fixed and fluctuating, as long as he shall live, or with his consent given during his life, or after his death, through one

in 1679 through the priests' being made unremovable,[1] was in part compensated for, in 1699, by his receiving the right of presentation of the curé in those parishes where the seigniors of fiefs had forfeited their rights as patrons.[2] While the curés were to be protected in the permanency of their

holding a canonry or prebend in the said Church of Quebec or other presbyter of the same; such canon, prebend, or presbyter to be approved by the future bishop, and the future bishop himself shall have power and legal right to full use, possession and enjoyment of all and single the privileges, honours, rights, distinctions, exemptions, liberties, immunities, favours, rewards, and indulgences, to the full use, possession, and enjoyment of which other bishops have full power and right by common law." (*Mandements*, vol. i, p. 82 *et seq.*)

[1] *Edits et Ord.* (1803), vol. i, p. 243.

[2] "In the petition presented to the King in Council by the Bishop of Quebec, reciting that His Majesty has hitherto granted to private individuals, to whom he has made grants of Fief in New France, the patronage of the churches of these fiefs, on the condition that these churches should be built of stone, but that, up to the present, most of these private individuals have shown no great desire to take advantage of the favor which His Majesty has been good enough to confer upon them, and that even the said bishop, who by right should be preferred to all others in having churches erected, has been prevented by these people from doing so, in some cases on the pretext that they are about to have them erected immediately themselves, and in other cases from a hesitation as to the location of their parishes—[all] which is contrary to the pious intentions of His Majesty, and prevents Divine Service being conducted with the proper decorum, and the inhabitants from receiving the spiritual assistance of which they have need:

"To the end that such evils be avoided, His Majesty in Council has ordained and doth ordain that the said bishop shall have power to build churches of stone in all the parishes and fiefs of New France not as yet provided with them, in situations which shall be judged the most suitable for the convenience of the inhabitants; in virtue of which action the bishop shall have the right of patronage of them [the churches], without, however, having the power to prevent the seigniors of the said parishes and fiefs from completing any churches under construction, or to prevent those who have collected the materials to build churches, from building them; and the patronage of these churches shall continue to be enjoyed by such persons as before the present decree." (*Ibid.*, pp. 292-293; *cf. ibid.*, pp. 244-245.)

cures and their revenues, nevertheless they were to keep within the law in collecting them.[1] They were expected by the king to use to the utmost their influence in strengthening the position of the state;[2] and any marked disloyalty was to be followed by removal.[3]

Even the character of the Canadian priesthood appears not to have passed unnoticed under the watchful eye of the king; for instructions were given that, on account of the independent and unreliable disposition of the Canadians, few of them should be received into orders.[4]

[1] Two priests who attempted to collect tithes on cattle as well as all products of the land were forbidden by the council to make any innovation. (*Jugements et Dél.*, vol. v, pp. 184-186.)

[2] ". . . being persuaded that you will urge them [the clergy] to do everything in their power to contribute at this juncture to maintain among the inhabitants a spirit of firm union, of fitting obedience, and of willingness to employ their means and their persons for their own preservation. This He expects from your piety, your prudence, and from your affectionate devotion to His service, more than from any other thing." (Minister to Saint-Vallier, *C. A.*, B. 16, pt. i, p. 137.)

[3] *Ibid.*

[4] "Having kept in mind the directions given to him before his departure, to make few Canadian priests, on account of their independent and unreliable disposition, He thinks that in order to follow out this counsel it would be advisable that he should be able to nominate to the vacant canonries some of the directors of the Seminary of Quebec, who can easily assist at all the offices of the chancel, and also fulfil the duties of their community. In this way there will not be at Quebec so many useless priests, who, for lack of sufficient occupation, begin to indulge in worldly amusements, gaming, feasting and dissoluteness. Owing to this idleness they think of nothing but wrangling, and sowing dissensions, both among themselves and amongst the laity; and some there are even who use language calculated to incite the people to independence and revolt. He purposes also to appoint to the chapter some of the old curés who, having worked zealously in their missions, and being no longer able to support the burden of them, would however be able to assist in the chancel, and to render more service to the people of Quebec than these young canons in whom they have no confidence, and who generally scandalize them. He has communicated

To summarize the various steps in the evolution of ecclesiastical control as dealt with in this chapter, it is necessary to recall both the forces favorable to the rise and development of ecclesiastical control and those unfavorable to it. As we have seen, among the forces favorable to the rise and development of this control were: the large place the conversion of the natives occupied in the minds of the early explorers and colonizers, the devoted character of the early missionaries, the astute leadership of the Jesuits in securing officials in harmony with their aims and ideals, the success of the missionaries as agents of the state among the Indians, the efficient leadership of Laval in unifying the ecclesiastical factions by bringing about the triumph of the Papal over the Gallican party, and the erection of the Archbishopric of Quebec directly subject to the See of Rome. Among the important forces mentioned as unfavorable to, and limiting the rise and development of, ecclesiastical control were: the new emphasis laid upon material prosperity under Colbert's and succeeding administrations, the recognition and acceptance of the Gallican principle that the king and not the pope was head of the church in all matters affecting the king's temporal dominion, and the contention that the ecumenical council and not the pope was supreme in all spiritual matters. We have seen also that the hostile attitude of the state toward the claims of the church soon brought about a determined resistance to the domination of the Roman Catholic hierarchy in the Sovereign Council, and, in addition, active interference by the state in such matters as tithes, religious houses, the public ministry of the church and numerous other clerical encroachments.

Thus under the French régime the state, from being the

this project to M. de Beauharnois, who has approved highly of it." (M. de Beauharnois and Hocquart to Conseil de Marine, June 17, 1730, *C. A.*, C^{11}, vol. cvi, p. 209.)

handmaid of the church, gradually became its master, and wielded the temporal sword with an iron hand. From the beginning of the rise of ecclesiastical control under the Jesuits until its challenge during the progressive administration of Colbert, theocratic influences predominated. For the remainder of French rule in Quebec, with the exception of the short term of Governor Denonville between the twc administrations of Frontenac, the influence of the church was more and more confined to the spiritual sphere.

CHAPTER V

Church and State under British Rule

The golden age of the Roman Catholic church in Quebec is to-day generally believed to have been during the French régime. That this is not warranted by the facts of history is shown by a comparison of the status of the church in the two periods, French and British. It was not until after the conquest by Great Britain in 1759, that the Roman Catholic church in Quebec received that legal status which is responsible for giving to it a control without parallel among the other Roman Catholic churches of the world.

This unique success is all the more remarkable when it is remembered that it was practically accomplished within the first half century of British rule; and this notwithstanding the policy of the British government to establish the Church of England, " both in principles and practice," in order that the new subjects should be brought up in those principles, and gradually embrace the Protestant religion. The religious settlement at the conquest made it clear that only a mere toleration of the Roman Catholic religion was intended by the articles of capitulation and the Treaty of Paris.

The success of the Roman Catholic church, however, would be difficult to explain if it were not that it was dealing with a population remarkable for its homogeneity and mental and moral unity.

All through the further historical treatment of our subject the importance of this fundamental fact must never be left out of account. Though the part played by social solidarity may not be emphasized in connection with every topic treated, its influence is always discernible. At bottom it is perhaps the most important of all those things which give significance to the events and conditions now about to be discussed. The events themselves are in many instances merely incidents which grew out of the attempts of the British government to adjust its policies to the existing social solidarity.

The growth of the control of the Roman Catholic church during the British régime was an inevitable result of that adjustment. Almost every important adjustment attempted by the British reacted to increase the power of the church. All through this chapter the careful reader will not overlook this point in connection with each of the topics treated. In the first place, he will note how, at first, after the conquest, the policies of the British military government were aimed at conciliating a thoroughly homogeneous people very different in type from the rulers. His attention will then be caught by the fact, that after the civil authorities began their administration, friction arose over the attempts of the British to accustom this homogeneous population of French Canadians to the English legal code. He will perceive further how this attempt at assimilation merely played into the hands of the Roman Catholic clergy by making them the natural leaders of the people in their opposition to the unworkable policies of the British. After the French civil authorities had returned to France there were none but the clergy to whom the people could turn for support against the policies they disliked. Later the reader will realize also how many concessions to the Roman Catholics had to be made by the government merely through fear lest the French Canadians might attempt to regain their French allegiance or to throw in their lot with the colonies to the

South. He will see also how inevitable it was that a Roman Catholic clergy should receive support from a solidly Roman Catholic people when the British attempted to establish the Church of England. He will appreciate also the influence of the presence of social solidarity in the separation of the Province of Quebec into Upper and Lower Canada and he will understand how inevitable it was that, after the extension of the franchise in 1791 had made the French Canadian population a highly important factor in determining questions of state, the political and social control of the Roman Catholic church in Quebec should have reached the practically supreme position which it now holds.

As has been said the first reaction of the British military government to the French Canadian population was one of conciliation. In fact whatever may have been the attitude of the New England colonists to their bitter enemies and trade rivals, the people of New France, the British Government on the whole was favorably disposed to its new subjects. It was said,

Far from experiencing at the moment of entire conquest, the dreadful effects of restraint and captivity, the virtuous general who conquered them made them feel the mildness of the British Government. . . . The mildness and forbearance of the conqueror has so firmly attached them to Your Excellent Majesty that their bonds are now become indissoluble and that they will be every day more strongly united.[1]

Their good was not only to be desired, but it was considered expedient to make them appreciate British rule. Their loyalty or even neutrality in the event of France attempting to regain her lost possession, was not to be lightly prized.

[1] *Tracts Relating to the American Stamp Act*, 1774, p. 67.

During the winter following the reduction of the province, the people, owing to the war and the poor harvest, would have suffered from famine, had it not been for the relief fund raised from the British population. Even the private soldiers gave a day's pay, or a day's provision in the month.[1]

In Colonel Burton's report of the state of the Government of Three Rivers, the peasantry in the open country seemed to appreciate the protection they received in the free exercise of their religion. "They begin to feel that they are no longer slaves, but that they do enjoy the full benefit of that indulgent and benign government." . . . [2] The government was extremely fortunate in having two men of such broad sympathy with the French Canadians, as General Murray and General Carleton. Hillsborough in a despatch to Carleton of March 1768 acknowledges this:

It gives me the greatest pleasure to acquaint you that His Majesty has been pleased to express the highest satisfaction in every part of your conduct, applauding very much your impartial and dispassionate attention to the public service in general, as well as the humanity and tenderness you have shewen with regard to the peculiar circumstances and situation of His Majesty's new subjects. . . . In the meantime, His Majesty wishes that His Canadian subjects should be assured of His gracious disposition to give them every mark of his royal protection that they can reasonably expect.[3]

In July of the same year we find another expression of the Government's desire to deal justly with its new subjects, and to overcome some of the abuses of the administration,

[1] General Murray's report, *Const. Docs.*, vol. i, p. 60.

[2] *Const. Docs.*, vol. i, p. 55.

[3] *C. A.*, Q. 5, pt. i, pp. 344-345.

It is His Majesty's firm purpose that every proper measure shall be taken to remedy those evils, and to remove the scandal and reproach brought upon His Majesty's Government, and the consequent unfavorable impressions made upon the minds of His Majesty's new subjects, which are the effects of the little attention given by the patentees in this kingdom to ability and integrity in the appointment of their deputies, and of the shameful frauds and exactions of exorbitant fees, which are practised, and of which you so justly complain. To this end I have received His Majesty's commands to lay your letters upon this subject before the Lords of Trade for their consideration, and to recommend such remedies as their Lordships shall judge best adapted to redress their grievances; and, in the meantime His Majesty trusts you will make some temporary arrangements to restrain the fees of office within some settled and certain bounds, so far as is right and the nature of the case will admit, and also with punishing with rigour those who shall be guilty of exaction or other malpractice in their offices.

These letters reveal a kindly disposition on the part of the conquerors to lighten the burdens of the conquered and to leave little doubt as to the paternal regard of Downing Street for the Canadians.

It was true that the Colonial Office was suspicious of the influence of the clergy. Egremont makes this clear in his instruction to Governor Murray, of August 13, 1763, a few months after the signing of the Treaty of Paris. Murray is warned to see that the free exercise of the Roman Catholic religion, which had been granted to the inhabitants, might not become a sinister instrument, fostering disloyalty in the event of an attempt to recover the country by France. Not only were the priests to be watched closely, but any who

[1] Hillsborough to the Governor of Quebec, *C. A.*, Q. 5, pt. ii, pp. 602-603.

busied themselves in the civil affairs were to be removed at once. In the fourth article of the treaty, which granted the "liberty of religion to the inhabitants of Canada," Egremont pointed out that such liberty was conditional, inasmuch as it was limited by a proviso, "As far as the laws of Great Britain will permit," followed by a rider, "which laws prohibit absolutely all Popish Hierarchy in any of the Dominions belonging to the Crown of Great Britain, and can only admit of a toleration of the exercise of that religion."

Egremont further states that this was clearly understood in the negotiations of the Treaty, for the French ministers had proposed to insert the word *comme ci devant* in order that the Roman Catholic religion should continue to be exercised in the same manner as under their government, and that they did not give up this point until it was made clear to them that the king had not the power to tolerate the Roman Catholic religion in any other manner than as far as the laws of Great Britain permitted.

The priests were to be watched closely. Only such priests and ecclesiastical persons as took the oath of allegiance were to be allowed to take up their residence. The emigration of regular clergy from France was to be discouraged, as well as the filling up of vacancies in the various religious orders.[1]

The articles of capitulation of Quebec and Montreal show that church matters occupied a large place in the peace negotiations. The French commander at Quebec, M. de Ramsey, requested that the free exercise of the Roman Catholic religion should be preserved, and that safeguards should be given to the houses of the clergy, to the monasteries, and equally to the Bishop of Quebec. The bishop was to be per-

[1] Egremont to General Murray, *C. A.*, Q. 1, p. 117 *et seq.*

mitted to reside permanently in his diocese, and to be free to exercise his functions as the dignity of the office required. These conditions were granted by General Townsend until such time as the possession of Canada should be decided upon by their respective governments.[1] The negotiations, as carried on by General Amherst and the Marquis of Vaudreuil, in the final capitulation at Montreal, are more detailed. There was to be granted free exercise of the Roman Catholic religion, which would permit the people to assemble in the churches and to frequent the sacraments without any interference. The request, that the people be obliged, by the English Government, to pay their tithes to the priest, was "left to the King's pleasure." The clergy, including the chaplain, priests, curates and missionaries, were "to continue with an entire liberty the exercise and functions of their cures in the parishes of the towns and country."

The grand vicars were to be permitted to administer a diocese during a vacancy in an episcopal see, and to be free to reside or visit in any parish. The extravagant demand that, in case Canada should remain under the British, the French king should retain the right to name the bishop was refused, together with the more moderate one, asking that he should always be of the Roman Catholic communion. The bishop, however, was given the right to establish new parishes and to provide for the rebuilding of his cathedral and his episcopal palace. He might reside in any parish, and visit in any part of his diocese with accustomed ceremonies. All the jurisdiction was to be accorded him, which had been exercised by his predecessors under the French régime, except that he might be called upon to take the oath of fidelity to do nothing contrary to the service of his British Majesty.

[1] Articles of capitulation agreed on between General Townsend and M. de Ramsey, Commander of Quebec. (*Annual Register*, 1759, p. 247, art. vi; *cf. Const. Docs.*, vol. i, p. 6.)

Among the religious orders, the nuns were to be preserved in their constitution and privileges. They were exempted from lodging any military officers or men, and to be afforded sufficient protection. These privileges were not to extend to the male orders of the Jesuits, *Récollets* and the house of priests of St. Sulpice at Montreal, until the king's pleasure should be known. All their real and personal property, however, was to be secured to them. Passage was to be provided in British vessels for all who wished to return to France, and they were to be allowed to dispose of or to take with them their chattels.[1] The report of General Murray showed the church to be well organized and prosperous. Of the total 7,985,470 acres of land granted in Canada by the French king, 2,043,790, or 25.6 per cent, was in possession of the church and religious orders. When it is remembered that nearly twenty-five per cent of all the land in France was in possession of the clergy, this proportion does not seem so large.[2] The Jesuits were the largest owners, having 881,695 acres.[3] The bishop had a stipend of 10,000 *livres*, 8,000 of which came from an endowment of Louis XIV, together with a grant of 2,000 *livres* from the clergy of France. He had no estate except his palace at Quebec, and a small property adjoining it.

The religious communities included the chapter of Quebec, consisting of one dean and twelve canons, the mendicant order of *Récollets* numbering ten; the Seminary of Quebec, an institute preparing students for orders with a staff of five; and the Jesuits, who numbered nine, and were in charge of two Indian missions. The communities of women included

[1] Articles of capitulation between General Amherst and Marquis de Vaudreuil. *Annual Register*, 1760, p. 222, arts. xxvii-xxxv; *cf. Const. Docs.*, vol. i, pp. 25-26.

[2] Duruy, p. 513.

[3] *C. A.*, Q. 56, pt. iii, p. 833.

those in the convent of the Hotel-Dieu, the General Hospital, as well as *Les Filles de la Congregation*; the two former being engaged in the care of the sick, while the latter did educational work among girls.

For four years after the articles of capitulation were signed the Province was under military rule and relationships between the French Canadians and the English officials were on the whole cordial. Trouble began in earnest when the civil authorities took the government over in 1764 and commenced to apply the provisions of English law. It had been hoped that the English law would prove even a greater factor in anglicizing Canada than had the conciliatory policies outlined in the last few pages. Edwin Burke was convinced of this, and stated in the British House of Commons, "In order to make Canada a secure possession of the British government, you have only to bind the people to you, by giving them your laws. Give them English liberty—give them an English constitution and then, whether they speak English or French, whether they go to mass, or attend our own communion, you will render them valuable and useful subjects of Great Britain." [1]

A general system of justice and administration had been established under the military rulers Amherst and Murray in 1760, and had been approved by the king through the Earl of Egremont, secretary of state, in a despatch to General Amherst, December 12, 1761.[2]

During this period of British military rule, the policy as has been said, was that of conciliation. Full consideration was given to the habits and customs of the new sub-

[1] Cavendish, p. 289.

[2] Commission as judge to Jacques Allier by Murray. *Const. Docs.*, vol. i, p. 30; Placard from His Excellency General Amherst, *ibid.*, p. 32; Ordinance Establishing Military Courts, *ibid.*, p. 35.

jects in the four years during which the final possession of Canada was still in doubt. By the Treaty of Paris, however, all was changed. Canada became a British dominion, and, as such, British institutions and law were made the basis for civil life.

On August 10, 1764, Civil Government was introduced, and on the 17th of September in the same year, the ordinance for the establishment of civil courts came into force. This ordinance laid down that the judges in both criminal and civil cases were "to determine agreeable to equity, but nevertheless having regard to the laws of England as far as circumstances and the present situation of things would admit, until such time as proper ordinances for the information of the people can be established by the Governor and the Council agreeable to the laws of England."[1] The French laws and customs were to be allowed and admitted only in cases between new subjects, where the cause of action had been brought before the first of October 1764. Canadian advocates, Proctors, etc., were to be allowed to practise.[2] Both old and new subjects were to be admitted on juries without distinction. The legal disqualification of Roman Catholics as jurors, General Murray had thought expedient to overlook until such time as the king's pleasure was known.[3] He justified this action on the ground that inasmuch as "There are but two hundred Protestant subjects in the Province, the greatest part of which are disbanded soldiers of little property and mean capacity, it is thought unjust to exclude the new Roman Catholic subjects to sit on juries, as such exclusion would constitute the said two

[1] *C. A.*, Q. 62a, pt. ii, p. 500; *cf.* also Ordinances Established in Civil Courts, *Const. Docs.*, vol. i, p. 149.

[2] *Ibid.*, p. 150.

[3] *Ibid.*, p. 149.

hundred Protestants perpetual judges of the lives and property of, not only the eighty thousand of the new subjects, but likewise of all the military in the Province; besides, if the Canadians are not to be admitted on juries, many will emigrate." [1] Two years later, this temporary expedient, was ratified by the Colonial Office. The English-speaking inhabitants were greatly incensed that the French-speaking subjects should be admitted as jurors on both grand and petty juries.[2] They looked upon this as an open violation of their most sacred laws and liberties, and as tending to the utter subversion of the Protestant religion. They believed the French-speaking subjects still to be under all the legal disabilities of the law of James I.[3] Protestants only were to be eligible for judges or justices of the peace. Owing to the few Protestants in the district of Three Rivers, such difficulty was experienced in securing suitable persons capable of acting as justices of the peace, that only two judicial districts, Quebec and Montreal, could be formed.[4]

The French Canadians, even although certain privileges had been granted, soon became dissatisfied with English law, and its administration. Its enforcement occasioned great confusion and embarrassment. Canadians were ignorant not only of English law and how they were to govern themselves in cases where the written laws gave no directions, but were utter strangers to the language in which these laws were written. The few who formed an exception, had only a smattering of the language of their conquerors.[5] The administrators of the law had almost as little knowl-

[1] *C. A.*, Q. 62a, pt. ii, p. 500.

[2] *Ibid.*, Q. 62a, pt. ii, p. 503.

[3] *Ibid.*, Dartmouth Papers, vol. i, p. 34 *et seq.*

[4] Ordinance Establishing Civil Courts. *Const. Docs.*, vol. i, p. 151.

[5] *Tracts Relating to the American Stamp Act*, p. 10; *cf.* Garneau, vol. ii, p. 408.

edge of French.[1] In Governor Murray's observations, he states that, " We have not yet got one English barrister or attorney who understands the French law." [2] Added to this mutual misunderstanding, the men who were charged with the administration of justice, were for the most part, incompetent. Too little care had been exercised in the choice of civil officers. Such officers as secretary of the province, registrar, clerk of the council, commissary of the stores and provisions, provost marshal, etc., were given by patent to men of political influence in England, who let them out to those paying the most. Not one of those who were actual administrators in close contact with the people understood any French.

Since these positions were without salary, the Governor had been instructed to allow the fees customary in the richest colonies. These, together with the exorbitant fees of the English lawyers, fell heavily upon the poor Canadians.[3]

Two of the leading officials, the chief justice and the attorney general, were so unqualified for their offices that they were both dismissed early in 1766.[4] They did not possess even a working knowledge of French; and their attitude towards the law seemed to be to make it as expensive and as cumbersome as possible for litigants.[5] The French Canadians fared no better at the hands of the magistrates. Governor Murray speaks of these as being chosen from " four hundred and fifty contemptible sutlers and traders, who were intoxicated with the unexpected power put into their hands, and eager to show how amply

[1] Dartmouth Papers, *C. A.*, M. 383, p. 172.

[2] *C. A.*, Q. 624, pt. ii, p. 504.

[3] Haldimand Collection, *C. A.*, B. 8, p. 1.

[4] *Ibid.; cf. C. A.*, Q. 3, pp. 1-4.

[5] Dartmouth Papers, *C. A.*, M. 383, p. 172.

they possess it. The Canadian *noblesse* were hated because their birth and their behaviour entitled them to respect, and the peasants were abhorred because they were saved from the oppression they were threatened with." [1]

During the first four years following the conquest, the Canadians had enjoyed peace and justice under the military administration. "Disinterestedness and equity" were felt to have characterized all its decisions. The civil administration, on the other hand, was the embodiment of misunderstanding, confusion and oppression. The French inhabitants felt the injustice of being expected to comprehend legal constructions put upon the law in a language that was unfamiliar to them. The English law of arrest and imprisonment for debt was especially offensive. Under the French law no action went against the person of the debtor until his chattels were found insufficient, and in the meantime, he was allowed to dispose of them to good advantage.[2]

The French Canadians also complained that whereas previously their family affairs had been settled at slight expense, now, the law had become so costly as to be ruinous to the debtor and of little value to the creditor. They accused certain officials and lawyers, not only with obstructing justice for their own profit, but also of being open to bribery.[3]

The Colonial Office, in order to avoid any misunderstanding of the Proclamation made in 1763 and enforced first in 1764, with regard to the status of the French-speaking inhabitants in the latter year, sent out the following instructions to Governor Murray:

[1] *C. A.*, B. 8, p. 1.

[2] *Tracts Relating to American Stamp Act*, p. 12 *et seq.*

[3] Haldimand Collection, *C. A.*, B. 8, p. 121; *cf.* also Cavendish, p. 107.

There shall extend to all subjects in general the protection and benefit of the British laws and constitution in all cases where their lives and liberties are concerned. But this shall not operate to take away from the native inhabitants the benefit of their own laws and customs in cases where Titles to Land, and the modes of Descent, Alienation and Settlement are in question. nor to preclude them from any share in the Administration of Judicature which both in Reason and Justice they are entitled to in common with the rest of our subjects.[1]

It took considerable time, however, for the Colonial Office to become fully aware of the general situation which had been created. In Hillsborough's letter to Carleton, he stated that "It was most unfortunate for the Colony of Quebec that weak, ignorant, and interested men were sent over to carry the Proclamation into execution, who expounded it in the most absurd manner, oppressive and cruel to the last degree, to the subjects, and entirely contrary to the Royal Intention."[2]

In the meantime although the report of Yorke and De Grey to the Privy Council had stated that they were not subject to the incapacities, disabilities and penalties which Roman Catholics were under in Great Britain;[3] still the repeated challenge of their rights and privileges by English subjects,[4] the uncertainty shown by those in authority with regard to these rights,[5] the confusion of the laws, the dilatory proceedings of the courts in a language they did not understand; together with the great expense attending them,[6]

[1] Dartmouth Papers, *C. A.*, M. 383, vol. i, p. 50.

[2] *C. A.*, Q. 5, pt. i, p. 344.

[3] Haldimand Collection, *C. A.*, B. 8, p. 12; *cf. Memoires sur le Canada*, p. 75; *A Pol. and Hist. Account of L. C.*, p. 115.

[4] Dartmouth Papers, *C. A.*, vol. i, p. 34.

[5] *C. A.*, Q. 63, pt. ii, p. 310.

[6] Maseres, *Collections of several commissions and other public instruments, etc.*, p. 50.

all contributed to develop and to foster in the Canadians a feeling of perplexity and alarm. Such references as these did much to make them apprehensive both of their political and their religious status in the future.

This apprehension was still further increased by the absence of civil leaders. The volume of emigration to France after the conquest without doubt was small. It included, however, a fairly large proportion of the leaders; the former government officials, the professional men and the wealthier merchants. These, however together with certain of the *noblesse* appear to have been the only persons who accompanied the troops to France. General Gage reported in 1762 that "no persons have left this Government to go to France, except Those who held Military and Civil Employments under the French king. . . . I perceive none preparing to leave the Government, or that seemed inclined to do so, unless it be a few Ladys whose Husbands are already in France. . . ."[1]

It is clear that the emigration after the conquest was drawn almost altogether from the influential classes in the towns and cities; the country population being little effected.[2] The result was that the French Canadians who had been nurtured under a paternal government, and who were most dependent upon the leadership of those in a higher station, were suddenly left without their accustomed leaders. At the same time they were subjected to all the perplexity and confusion already outlined in this chapter, which attended the attempt of the British authorities to introduce English law and customs. The outcome of this situation was that a strong feeling of fear was developed among the French Canadians. The belief developed that the Proclamation of October 7, 1763, was aimed,

[1] *Const. Docs.*, vol. i, p. 72.

[2] *C. A.*, Q. 2, pp. 98-99.

At once to abolish all the usages and customs of Canada, with the rough hand of conquerer rather than with the true spirit of a lawful Sovereign, and not so much to extend the protection and benefit of His English laws to His new subjects, by securing their lives, liberties and properties with more certainty than in former times, as to impose new, unnecessary and arbitrary rules, especially in the Titles to Land, and in the modes of Descent, Alienation and Settlement, which tend to confound and subvert rights, instead of supporting them.[1]

In an "Ordinance for quieting People in their Possessions" . . . of November 6, 1764, it was stated that, "It appears right and necessary, to quiet the Minds of the People, in Regard to their Possessions, and to remove every doubt respecting the same." [2] The uncertainty as to the future of religion increased still further this element of fear. The French Canadians acknowledged gratefully the fact that they enjoyed "The same happiness and tranquillity in their religion," as under the old régime [3] but there was grave doubt as to whether, with the increase of the English population, the free exercise of their religion might not be gradually withdrawn. The attitude of some of the English-speaking subjects tended to increase this feeling.[4] Cramahe, in writing on this point, to Hillsborough, remarks that "they have at times been likewise alarmed upon this head by the indiscreet talk of some individuals amongst us." [5]

The clergy, especially the better trained among them, had

[1] Report of Attorney and Solicitor General regarding the Civil Government of Quebec. Dartmouth Papers, *C. A.*, M. 383, vol. i, p. 172 *et seq.*

[2] *Const. Docs.*, vol. i, p. 166; *cf.* also *Ordinances made for the Province of Quebec, by the Governor and Council, etc.*, p. 18.

[3] *C. A.*, B. 8, p. 121.

[4] Dartmouth Papers, *C. A.*, vol. i, pp. 31, art. vii, 34 *et seq.*

[5] *C. A.*, Q. 8, p. 162.

been largely drawn from France.[1] After the conquest their further immigration was discouraged. This soon led to a lack of priests to fill the vacancies and occasioned further anxiety on the part of the inhabitants. Murray writes in his letter to Halifax, "They must certainly have conceived some uneasiness at the words of the treaty, and allege their fears are not for themselves but for their children, if no provision is made to supply the priesthood, as vacancies happen." [2]

It was natural for the Canadians under this social pressure of fear to appeal to their own native leaders. Under the French régime, these would have been the officials, professional classes, and the wealthier merchants. Now only the less influential of the last two classes remained. There was still, however, another powerful group of leaders, the clergy, who up to this time, had never been recognized by the Canadians as possible leaders in securing greater justice. For a century previous to the conquest, the king and Superior Council had sought rather to protect the people through limiting the privileges and prerogatives of the clergy than through extending them. Their great influence in the state, had been used so largely to retain their ecclesiastical position that the people had not looked to them for civil leadership.

In the absence of their accustomed leaders the fear of losing their laws and religion under the early British administration, however, compelled the people to turn to the clergy for leadership. In this crisis the people and the clergy had much in common.

The French laws and customs were dear to the hearts of the Canadians. The legalizing of the tithes meant much to the clergy. The free exercise of religion was held of

[1] *Const. Docs.*, vol. i, p. 54.

[2] *C. A.*, Q. I, pp. 251-252.

supreme importance by both priest and people. The growing discontent proved the clergy's opportunity. Through a new alliance with the people and by championing the cause of the people in the struggle to retain their laws and customs the clergy not only obtained, the right to tithes, but also gained tremendously in unity and control.

The fear of French influence and intrigue soon further narrowed this new leadership practically to Canadian-born clergy. This followed the action of the British Government, which in order to minimize the danger from France, excluded all foreign ecclesiastics of the House of Bourbon from Canada. In this way it was hoped to prevent the church from becoming a centre for arousing French sentiment in Canada.[1]

As early as 1768, Hillsborough had written to Carleton approving of his plan of giving every preference to the Canadian-born clergy, and instructing him to discourage "the introduction of foreign priests,"[2] as the government would soon consider their complete exclusion.[3] While this plan was strongly approved by the officials in Canada they saw at the same time that it was most likely to prejudice the French-born clergy in favor of a return to French rule.[4]

[1] "I am persuaded that the most effectual way of securing the attachment of the Canadians is that of preventing by all possible means every communication or connection with France, or persons who are influenced in favor of that country, and therefore it behooves the king's servants to be watchful of their conduct, upon every occasion and to act with great firmness whenever any discovery should be made of even an attempt inconsistent with their entire separation." (Sydney to Haldimand, *C. A.*, B. 45, p. 130; *cf.* Egerton, *A Short History of British Colonial Policy*, p. 236.)

[2] *C. A.*, Q. 4, p. 321; Q. 5, pt. i, p. 345; Q. 12, A., p. 4.

[3] *Ibid.*

[4] "It is not indeed improbable that the French clergy, jealous of their Canadian brethren, for whom they have always had a thorough con-

The desire of the British officials to minimize the influence of those of the clergy who were most closely attached in sympathy, to France and the old régime, had the effect, in the end of strengthening the leadership of the Canadian-born clergy over the people. This effort, to lesson the influence of the sympathizers with the old régime was particularly strong after the American Revolutionary War.[1] The action of the Catholic clergy during the American Revolutionary War on the whole had been highly commendable. It was thought, however, by some that when the part France had taken in the war became known that a change in the attitude of some of the clergy became noticeable. Haldimand wrote to Germain that,

However sensible I am of the good conduct in general during the invasion of the province in the year 1775 I am well aware that since France was known to take a part in the contest, and since the address of the Count D'Estaing and a letter of Mons. de la Fayette to the Canadians and Indians has been circulated in the province, many of the priests changed their opinions and in the case of another invasion would, I am afraid, adopt another system of conduct.[2]

The entrance of France into the war naturally had awakened hopes in some members of the clergy that Canada might be returned to France at the Treaty of Paris.[3] The disap-

tempt and whom they now see likely to become in time possessed of every benefice in their church . . . would be desirous to bring about a change." (Cramhé to Hillsborough, *C. A.*, Q. 8, p. 162.)

[1] Haldimand to Germain, Haldimand Papers, *C. A.*, B. 56, p. 76; *cf. C. A.*, Q. 16, pt. ii, p. 689.

[2] *C. A.*, B. 54, p. 340.

[3] "I observe great disappointment on the part of some of the clergy, on occasion of Canada's not returning by the Treaty of Peace, under the Dominion of France. I have found a greater reluctance on Mr. Montgolfier to part with the two French priests mentioned in my

pointment of these led Haldemand to believe that it was "more than ever incumbent upon the government in the country to be vigilant, against the machinations of France and the American Congress." [1]

In the case of the French-born curé De la Valiniere, Haldimand had taken drastic action in ordering his arrest and deportation.[2] In the spring of 1783 two French priests, attired in "secular habit" had found passage on one of the merchant vessels and on their arrival had been permitted by the bishop to proceed to Montreal.[3] As they had failed to report themselves to the governor, notwithstanding the request of the bishop and citizens of Montreal that they be allowed to become attached to the Seminary, Haldimand insisted upon their immediate departure for Europe.[4] In order to prevent any such recurrence the governor announced "His Majesty's determination and orders relative to the admission of foreign ecclesiastics into the province and the total exclusion of any priests from France or other countries under the dominion of the House of Bourbon." [5]

This measure did not aim at reducing the number of the clergy, for the government in response to petitions from the people praying that priests might be brought from Europe,[6]

public letter than I had reason to expect from his former good conduct or the circumstances of the case. The war has ended so unfortunately for us that people begin to think slightly of our power, and it is the general opinion that if France had insisted upon it Canada would have been added to them." (Haldimand to Lord North, *C. A.*, B. 56, p. 77.)

[1] *C. A.*, B. 56, p. 76; *cf. ibid.*, B. 56, p. 97; *C. A.*, Q. 79, pt. i, p. 204.

[2] *C. A.*, Q. 16, p. 2, pp. 689, 690; *cf. ibid.*, p. 175; *C. A.*, Q. 17, pt. i, p. 80.

[3] *C. A.*, B. 56, p. 75.

[4] *C. A.*, B. 56, pp. 75-76, 78, 96; *C. A.*, Q. 45, pt. ii, p. 512.

[5] *C. A.*, Q. 23, p. 370; *cf. C. A.*, Q. 45, pt ii, p. 512.

[6] "We are, Most Gracious Sovereign, in most urgent need of priests to carry on the work of the seminaries and missions of our province;

had authorized the admission of "any number of ecclesiastics that were necessary for supplying the vacant parishes in Canada and such other persons as they might judge proper for the tuition of their children, from any country not connected with the House of Bourbon." [1] The offer made by the government to secure Savoyard priests although at first refused by the bishop,[2] was accepted later and a few priests were sent out to Canada at the government's expense.[3]

The number of foreign-born clergy entering the country must have been small for, notwithstanding the number of inadequately prepared students who received orders,[4] continuous complaint was made of the scarcity of priests. Bishop Hubert wrote to Cardinal Antonelli in 1788,

directors and professors of this class, and indeed of any other, are lacking. Our colleges are deserted; from this want arises ignorance, and from ignorance, moral depravity. Submissive and loyal, this people hope to receive from Your Royal Clemency permission to bring from Europe persons of this class." (Petition of the Roman Catholic Citizens to the King, *C. A.*, Q. 62a, pt. i, p. 298; *cf. C. A.*, Q. 42, p. 138.)

[1] *C. A.*, B. 45, p. 130.

[2] *C. A.*, Q. 45, pt. ii, p. 512.

[3] "In consequence of the application made to the court of Turin, at your desire, for four Savoyard priests to fill the vacant benefices in Canada, Messrs. Majson, Bejson, du Clos and Bosson have arrived here, with the fullest testimonies of their life and attention to the duties of their sacred functions, and they now proceed to Quebec in the Amazon store ship, in which a passage has been provided for them and the master paid for sustaining them on the voyage. The incomes promised them, in consequence of your letter, is £200 a year each, at least, and they have received according to that allowance from their departure from Savoy to the 20th of this month, the day of their embarkation. You will only have to pay them from that day until you put them in possession of their benefices." (Shelbourne to Haldimand, *C. A.*, B. 45, p. 22; *cf. ibid.*, pp. 119, 130; Q. 42, p. 138; C. *A.*, B. 54, p. 342.)

[4] *C. A.*, B. 54, p. 341.

I have observed on my pastoral visitations the firm faith and attachment of our people to our Holy Religion, but it is to be feared that this good attitude on their part may be weakened by the scarcity of clergy, who are not sufficiently numerous to overtake the regular instructions of the people on account of the large territory to be traversed. In the diocese of Quebec there are only one hundred and forty priests, which is quite insufficient for an immense population which is so scattered as this is. Most of the priests are Canadian, and soon all will be, as the British Ministry does not permit the admission of European clergy, least of all Frenchmen. Its opposition on this point, manifested on several occasions, confines the diocese to priests which it can train itself, and this is a very mediocre resource.[1]

So successful had the British policy of exclusion been that the report of the Catholic clergy for 1790 showed that of the total of 149 clergy including the bishops, 132 or 88.7 per cent were native born.[2] The rigid enforcement of these regulations, it is true, was soon relaxed. From time to time a few French-born priests were admitted but under such restrictions that they never again became the dominating factor among the clergy.[3]

[1] *C. A.*, M. 128, p. 348 *et seq.*

[2] *C. A.*, Q. 48, pt. ii, p. 608.

[3] "Application has recently been made to me on the part of the Roman Catholic Bishop of Quebec concerning the further admission of French Emigrant Priests into this Province; from which I understand that in consequence of my letter (No. 14) of the 20th of October last your Grace has refused Passports to some of the Emigrant Clergy who were desirous of coming over here. . . . Upon this subject it is but justice to observe that the admission of any considerable number of the Emigrant Clergy into the Province can hardly fail of interfering with the views of those Canadians who seek ecclesiastical preferment for themselves or their children, and on this consideration alone (were there no other) I should think it my duty to recommend that very few more than those who have already obtained Passports be hereafter

This policy, although primarily political, was of far-reaching consequence to the unity of the clergy and the control of the church. The exclusion of French ecclesiastics cut off all contact with the Gallican church and the revolutionary movements in France. The dominant element among the clergy for the first time became Canadian. Thus the church and the people were compelled to depend upon a native clergy, who had practically no contact with the outside world, and whom the bishop considered "a mediocre source."[1] This opinion which seems to have been shared by other writers. Murray in describing the clergy wrote that "most of the dignified among them are French, the rest Canadians and are in general of the lower class of the people."[2] Haldimand pointed out that "the *Noblesse* and the better class of Canadians were never fond of embracing an ecclesiastical life."[3]

One of the results of this policy of minimizing the influence of adherents of the old régime was that the rivalry between the French and Canadian-born clergy and the contempt of the former for the latter, which had been a source of weakness, was overcome.[4] The native clergy, though

admitted. . . . In a political point of view I may add, it is perhaps to be apprehended, notwithstanding the present situation of affairs, that the introduction of these persons may, at some future period, become the means of forming a Bond of Connexion between the Canadas and France, or at least that it will prevent the remembrance of their former connexion from dying away in the minds of the Canadians. (Prescott to Portland, 1799, *C. A.*, Q. 79, pt. i, pp. 204-205; *cf. C. A.*, G. 9, p. 231.)

[1] "The priests of this country are generally good. They all wear clerical garments, and celebrate Mass every day. Little gross and scandalous vice is found amongst them: they are attached to their bishops, who in turn are attached to them." (Bishop Hubert to Cardinal Antonelli, *C. A.*, M. 128, p. 349 *et seq.*

[2] *Const. Docs.*, vol. i, p. 59.

[3] *C. A.*, B. 54, p. 341; *C. A.*, Q. 8, p. 163.

[4] *C. A.*, Q. 8, p. 162.

less learned, through their more intimate knowledge of the *habitants* gradually exerted larger and larger influence over them, a fact which became of immense importance later when the people were granted full political rights.

The church, however, could never have gained its position of authority after the conquest had it not been for the legal status granted to it by the British government. This was accomplished very largely through the passing of the Quebec Act in 1774, and the Constitutional Act in 1791.

In the royal proclamation of 1763 promises were held out that as soon as conditions warranted, legislation would be forthcoming to meet the needs of the new colony.[1] As early as 1770, Hillsborough wrote to Cramaché, "I have the satisfaction to acquaint you that the affairs of the province of Quebec are now under consideration of His Majesty's servants and that there is a prospect that such arrangements will speedily be made as will (I trust) lead to the removal of those difficulties and obstructions in the government of it which have been so long complained of." [2] In 1773, the situation appears to have become exceedingly difficult, for Cramaché wrote to Dartmouth, "I most sincerely wish for the good of the king's service and the happiness of the people matters may be soon brought to a final conclusion." [3]

Various petitions and memorials to the king and ministers from both the old and new subjects had been forwarded to London. The old subjects prayed for the granting of a "general assembly," [4] and the new subjects for having

[1] *Const. Docs.*, vol. i, pp. 119-123.

[2] *C. A.*, Q. 7, p. 267; *cf. C. A.*, Q. 8, p. 53.

[3] *C. A.*, Q. 9, p. 51; *cf. C. A.*, Q. 9, p. 157.

[4] *Const. Docs.*, vol. i, pp. 347-348; *cf. ibid.*, pp. 291-292, 349-351, 351-352.

their "ancient laws, privileges and customs restored" and their province extended "to its former boundaries." [1]

The task of the British legislators in framing an Act which would satisfy at once both the English and French Canadians was difficult indeed. They realized that it would be impossible to stamp out the Roman Catholic religion. Not only had they the advice of the best legal authorities but they had two precedents to guide them in dealing with a Roman Catholic population namely, Ireland and Minorca. "Ireland showed clearly that Catholicism could not be stamped out in Canada even with a population of Catholics of five to two, much less five hundred to one as in Canada. Minorca on the other hand where a lenient policy had been in force with a Roman Catholic people showed that even when England had been at war on two different occasions with Spain the people of Minorca, although Spaniards, had remained loyal to England." [2]

At the time therefore when the hand of the state was being forced by external pressure, when the fear of France coupled with that of the American colonies made the loyalty or neutrality of the French Canadians essential to the British at any price, the policy of conceding to the French Canadians their "ancient laws, privileges, and customs," was not only what "benevolence and humanity recommended" but also it was "consonant with the soundest policy." [3]

It would be unfair to the British Parliament to suggest that in the Quebec Act political expediency was a larger determining factor than "benevolence and humanity." Edwin Burke in his speech in Parliament while strongly opposed to the boundaries of Quebec being extended to

[1] *Const. Docs.*, vol. i, pp. 355-356; *cf. ibid.*, pp. 293-294, 358-359.

[2] *Tracts, Am. S. A.*, p. 19.

[3] *Ibid.*; *cf.* Dartmouth to Cramahé, *C. A.*, Q. 8, p. 221.

take in any English-speaking subjects, vigorously maintained,

> There is but one healing Catholic principle of toleration which ought to find favor in this House. It is wanted not only in our colonies, but here. The thirsty earth of our country is gasping and gaping, and crying out for the healing shower from heaven. The noble Lord has told you of the right of those people by treaty; but I consider the right of conquest so little and the right of human nature so much, that the former had had little consideration with me. I look upon the people of Canada as coming, by the dispensation of God, under the British government. I would have us govern it, in the same manner as the all-wise disposition of Providence would have us govern it. We know he suffers the sun to shine upon the righteous and the unrighteous; and we ought to suffer all classes, without distinction, to enjoy equally the right of worshipping God, according to the light He has been pleased to give them.[1]

Fears were expressed and with some justification that the bill would establish " the popish religion " in Quebec.[2] The question as to whether or not the clergy should be upheld in their legal right to tithes as they were under the French régime occasioned much debate. It is true no request had come from the French Canadians asking that this privilege be incorporated in the bill[3] although it appears to have been generally known among the people at the time that they were at liberty to pay or refuse to pay their tithes as they liked.[4] Carleton, on being questioned in Parliament ex-

[1] Cavendish, p. 222.

[2] *Ibid.*, p. 251.

[3] Maseres, . . . *Proceedings of the . . . Protestant Inhabitants . . . of Quebec . . . to Obtain an House of Assembly* . . . , p. 180.

[4] *Ibid.*

pressed the opinion that during this period the tithes were being paid as well as formerly.[1]

After much discussion the bill, however was finally passed by a vote of fifty-six to twenty, and received the royal assent June 22, 1774. The Quebec Act has sometimes been called the *magna charta* of French Canadian liberties for it secured to the Roman Catholics the right to "have, hold, and enjoy, the free Exercise of the Religion of the Church of Rome," and to their clergy the right to "hold, receive, and enjoy, their accustomed Dues and Rights, with respect to such Persons only as shall profess the said Religion.[2] Moreover the Act substituted for the "statute passed in the First Year of the Reign of Queen Elizabeth or any other Oaths," a special oath of allegiance freed from any religious requirements.[3] The new subjects, the religious Orders and Communities only excepted, were also to be permitted to hold and enjoy their Property and Possessions, together with all Customs and Usages relative thereto, and all other Civil Rights consistent with their allegiance.[4]

The concessions granted in the Quebec Act to the French Canadians, and more especially to their clergy in legalizing

[1] Cavendish, p. 103.

[2] The Quebec Act, *Anno Decimo Quarto Georgii III, Regis*, cap. lxxxiii, cited in *Const. Docs.*, vol. i, p. 403.

[3] "I, A. B., do sincerely promise and swear, That I will be faithful, and bear true allegiance, to His Majesty King George, and him will defend to the utmost of my power against all traitorous Conspiracies, and Attempts whatsoever which shall be made against His Person, Crown and Dignity; and I will do my utmost Endeavor to disclose and make known to His Majesty, His Heirs and Successors all Treasons, and traitorous Conspiracies, and Attempts which I shall know to be against Him, or any of them; and all this I do swear without any Equivocation, mental Evasion, or secret Reservation, and renouncing all Pardons and Dispensations from any power or Person whomsoever to the contrary. So Help Me God." (*Ibid.*)

[4] The Quebec Act, *Const. Docs.*, vol. i, pp. 403-404.

tithes, were very possibly a bid, in part at least, for the loyalty and support of the French Canadians, in event of difficulties with France or the American Colonies.

When the break did come the following year the response from the clergy was most complete and the whole weight of their influence was thrown on the side of British rule.[1] It is said the hierarchy from the very beginning of British rule "foresaw that religion might profit by this change of masters" and this may have accounted in part for the attitude taken.[2] In 1759 the bishop addressed a letter to the parish priests giving them detailed instruction as to the prudence expected of those whose parishes might fall into the enemy's hands.[3] The following year the bishop wrote to Briand, the vicar general, "You cannot too earnestly enjoin upon the parish priests to be as prudent as possible. We must not meddle with temporal affairs. Our sole concern should be spiritual and then I am persuaded that General Murray will be satisfied."[4]

There could be no neutral ground, however, for the Roman Catholic church in the American Revolutionary War even if it had not been favorable to British rule. The New England colonists were looked upon by the hierarchy, as standing for the antithesis of Roman Catholicism and as the most blasphemous of the enemies of the church. Bishop Briand in his famous *mandement* "To Rebellious Subjects during the American War" upbraids them and laments the fact,

if God had not exercised His mercy, you would shortly have

[1] *Tracts, Am. S. A.*, p. 72.

[2] *Can. and its Prov.*, vol. ii, *New France* ii, p. 442.

[3] *Ibid.*, p. 441.

[4] *Ibid.*

become apostates, schismatics, and pure heretics, Protestants of a Protestantism the furthest removed from the Roman religion, and its cruelest enemy. For no other sect has persecuted the Romans like that of the Bostonians, no other has outraged the priests, profaned the churches, and the relics of the saints as it has, no other has attacked the confidence of Catholics in the protection of the Saints and of the Holy Mother of God with more horrible blasphemies as it has done. . . . No, my brethren, there is no doubt that very soon by their lies, by their calumnious tricks against your religion, by their deceitful sophistries, they would, not only have weaned you from that faith, but I do doubt not that they would even have finally succeeded in making you deplore the lot of your fathers, and that of your early years. You would soon have been heard chanting canticles of thanksgiving for having been delivered from the alleged superstitions of popery, and for having finally discovered the beautiful truth.[1]

Coupled with this distrust and hatred of the "Romans" for the "Bostonians," however, was the hierarchy's satisfaction with British rule. The bishop in the same *mandement* makes this clear when he reproaches the people for their ingratitude.

[1] Mandements aux sujets rebelles durant la guerre Américaine, *Mandements,* vol. ii, p. 269 *et seq.* There is further written in the same pastoral letter: "No, my dear brethren, the colonists in no way desired your welfare; it was by no means a fraternal affection that brought them to this colony; it was not at all to procure for you a liberty which you were already enjoying so advantageously, and which was about to become still more glorious, that a handful of men, neither warriors nor men instructed in military science, came to possess themselves of your farms and of the undefended Cities of Montreal and Three Rivers. It was because of a very different principle, on which, if you understood it thoroughly, would cover you with shame and disgrace, one which, if you could penetrate all its import, all its malice and treachery, would arouse you to rage and fury against these perfidious enemies whom you have had the folly to call by the name of brothers, friends, and 'our people'." *Ibid.*

Your rebellion . . . has already merited exemplary and rigorous chastisements on the part of a prince from whom you have, up to the present, received only signal marks of a generosity extraordinarily rare in a powerful conqueror, which none of us expected, generosity which has made you aware of the change of government only by a happier state of existence. No one, at the time of your revolt, felt any unhappy results from the late war. Whatever disorder it had caused at first in your affairs, was not only repaired, but you had besides greatly augmented your fortunes, and your possessions had become considerably more lucrative and more valuable. You had then, only cause to thank God for your lot. Duty and gratitude should have attached you inviolably to your sovereign, to His authority, and to His glory; He had the right to claim it, He even expected it with a certain degree of assurance; and he would not have been deceived, if you had followed the dictates of gratitude and the principles of your religion.

It was on this principle that, to constrain rebellious provinces to duty, and to bring them back to obedience, he was not afraid to withdraw from among us the troops which were believed to be no longer necessary to assure your submission, which indeed, one might with some foundation, believe to be engraved on your minds and hearts. It was expected, and reasonably that you would be eagerly assuming the interests and the defences of your beneficient king, of a Court and a Parliament entirely devoted to you, and completely occupied with plans to make you happy, rich and flourishing. What must have been the surprise of England when she heard of your defection, of your disobedience, of your revolt, and of your alliance with rebellious spirits. But what also must be her anger and indignation towards you. Have you not reason to fear that her mistaken kindness will turn into wrath, and that she will overwhelm you with punishment in place of the favors which she has heaped upon you up to the present, and which she was ready to accord in a still more extensive special and peculiar manner. Perhaps if the display of a part of her formidable forces had opened your eyes and recalled you to your duty, she would have excused you on account of your ignorance and simplicity, on account of the impositions, the tricks and falsehoods, the shams, the threats, and the false promises, preposterous and without basis, which your insidious enemies have employed to seduce you, to pervert you, and to engage you in their iniquitous designs, not through love for you and your well-being, but through envy and jealousy of the preferences which were being accorded to you.[1]

The bishop still further used his episcopal office in support of the British cause, for some of the French Canadian rebels were compelled to do penance for their political offence. It is recorded that on the occasion of the anniversary of the deliverance of Quebec from the American troops, the bishop personally conducted the great thanksgiving service when, "Eight unfortunate Canadians who had sided with the rebels were present, with ropes about their necks, and were forced to do penance before all in the church, and crave pardon of their God, Church and King."[2]

The loyalty of the hierarchy and especially of Bishop Briand in this crisis was appreciated by the British government, and greatly strengthened the control of the Roman Catholic church. Numerous instances of this appreciation might be mentioned. The following letter from Sydney to Hamilton, expressing regret at the resignation of Bishop Briand, is a good illustration.

From the long and faithful services of Mons. Briand, superintendent of the Romish Church in the province of Quebec, and the unblemished character which he possesses, you cannot be surprised the king accepted of his resignation with concern, especially upon observing the reasons which produced

[1] *Mandements*, vol. ii, p. 269 *et seq.*

[2] *Revolutionary Letters*, pp. 66-67.

it. His Majesty has in consequence commanded me to signify to you His Royal approbation that the Reverend Louis Philippe D'Esgly, should succeed to office in full confidence he will follow the virtuous example of Mons. Briand.[1]

It is true the British Government for a time did not officially recognize the "Superintendent of the Roman Catholic church" as bishop; nevertheless so satisfactory appears to have been the understanding between the government and the bishop that he was permitted to attend to the affairs of the church, even in matters where the formal consent of the government had not been received.[2]

However grateful the Government may have felt toward the hierarchy, it had no intention of changing a policy of mere toleration, to one of building up the Roman Catholic church. On the contrary the American Revolutionary War had still further confirmed its policy of establishing the Church of England as the national church.

[1] *C. A.*, Q. 24, p. 216; *cf.* Murray to Shelbourne, *C. A.*, Q. I, p. 261.

[2] "I have had the satisfaction to find that Lord Dorchester, Governor General of the Province, in the name of His Britannic Majesty, enters most graciously into my views. . . . For these reasons, after thanking Heaven for this, I take the liberty to implore your Eminence to intercede with His Holiness that he may crown this good work in permitting by an Apostolic Brief that *Messire* Charles François Bailly de Messein be consecrated as my coadjutor, under such title '*in partibus infidelium*' as it may please His Holiness to bestow upon him. . . . It will, perhaps, be a cause of surprise to the Roman Curia to note the absence of a formal document attesting the consent of the English Government in favor of M. Bailly. There will, perhaps, be found in our manner of proceeding in this way a lack of formality, and again perhaps it may appear singular that I should have addressed myself directly to His Eminence the Cardinal Prefect of the Propaganda, without regard to the precautions customary in such cases; but my answer is: 1st, that in such matters nothing but verbal statements can be expected on the part of the English Government, the formal approbation of a Catholic Bishop being entirely foreign, and even contrary to the spirit of the British constitution. . . ." (Bishop Hubert to Cardinal Antonelli, June 19, 1788, *C. A.*, M. 128, pp. 352-353.)

The want of a strong national church in the American colonies was considered to have been responsible in a measure for the rapid growth of democracy and the ultimate break with the motherland. The determination on the part of the British Ministry to avoid any such repetition of events in Quebec readily enlisted their support for the establishment of the Church of England in the colony. After the American Revolution, therefore, the policy of the government aimed more than ever to make Canada thoroughly English. Both the old and new subjects of his Majesty were to be anglicized. They were to be English first, not British; Anglican, not Protestant. Canada was to be made not a New England, but an orthodox England.

With slight modifications, the policy outlined in the instructions to General Murray for bringing this about through the establishment of the Church of England and the erecting of a system of public schools directly under the control of the Bishop of London and the governor, was to be carried out.[1]

[1] The instructions to General Murray stated explicitly that, in order that the Church of England might be established "both in principles and practice," and the new subjects be induced to embrace by degrees the Protestant religion and their children brought up in its principles, Protestant schools were to be erected. The cost of maintaining these, as well as providing for the support of the clergy, would be met by allotting for that purpose "proper quantities of land." Suggestions were to be made by Murray as to any further means by which he might consider the Protestant religion would "be promoted, established and encouraged" in the Province. (*C. A.*, Q. 26b, p. 26, art. xxxiii.) It was to be his special care to see that the worship of the Church of England was conducted with dignity and fitting solemnity. No Protestant minister was to be preferred to any living without a certificate from the Bishop of London "of his being conformable to the doctrines and discipline of the Church of England." (*Ibid.*, p. 27, art. xxxv.) Murray had the further right of "full power and authority to Collate any person or persons to any Churches, Chappels, or other Ecclesiastical Benefices within our said Province, as often as any of them shall happen to be void." (Commission of Captain-General and Governor-in-Chief of the Province of Quebec, *Const. Docs.*, vol. i, p. 126.)

Many difficulties, however, stood in the way of a "proper establishment of the Church of England." The French Canadians were not easily to be induced to accept the Protestant religion. The English population was a mere handful; more than a decade after the conquest, Sir Guy Carleton testified in the House of Commons that the estimated Protestant population in Quebec was "about 360 men, with women and children." [1] Even as late as 1789, in a letter to the Archbishop of Canterbury, Bishop Inglis wrote, "At Quebec there are but few English." [2] "The Canadians were to the English as five to one." [3] He further mentions having visited Three Rivers, "where there are about twenty-four Protestant families, and a Protestant settlement of fifteen families at River Du Loup." [4] In addition there was lacking able leadership and proper organization. The attempt to unite the English and Huguenots under a foreign clergy who had little knowledge of the liturgy of the Church of England, and less of the English language, coupled with the humiliation of holding service in a Roman Catholic church, all worked together to create an atmosphere unfavorable to the growth, and unfitting the dignity, of a national church.

For these reasons among others, the early progress of the Church of England was slow. In the absence of regular clergy certain foreign Protestant clergy had been appointed under commission from the governor to act in the capacity of curates,[5] in Quebec, Montreal and Three Rivers.[6] The

[1] Cavendish, *op. cit.*, p. 103.

[2] *Canadian Archives Report*, 1912, *Correspondence and Journals of Bishop Inglis*, p. 232.

[3] *C. A.*, M. 914, p. 154.

[4] *Canadian Archives Report*, 1912, *op. cit.*, p. 232.

[5] *C. A.*, Q. 5, pt. ii, p. 759.

[6] *Ibid.*, Q. 26, pt. i, p. 22.

Bishop of London, in a letter of September 29, 1768, seems to suggest some doubt as to the wisdom of this step when he says, "I suppose there can be no objection to the commissions which the governor has given to the ministers, to officiate as curates in such churches or places as the governor may appoint . . . it is all we can hope for until a more perfect establishment is made in the province." [1]

Although the need in a new country, no doubt, justified the governor in appointing certain ministers in the colony as curates, and justified the bishop in sanctioning their appointment, the church made little progress under their ministry. Some of the ministers at least, appear to have been of mean station and mediocre ability. In a letter on the state of the Church of England and the Clergy, the author writes,

What opinions must the Canadians form of our religion when they daily see the minister of it degrading the very name by keeping a little dirty dram-shop and himself so scandalously indecent, as to measure out and sell rum to the soldiers of the garrison, and all this too in the capital of the province, the seat of the government, and the residence of the French Bishop and other dignified clergy of that church? [2]

Other letters of the period, although less severe in their arraignment of the Protestant clergy, make it clear that many of them were quite unsuitable.[3] Haldimand, in re-

[1] *Ibid.*, Q. 5, pt. ii, p. 759.

[2] *C. A.*, Q. 26, pt. i, p. 59. "Upon the whole, from an attentive but painful observation of our religious concerns in this province for ten years past, it may with safety be pronounced that unless our church is put upon a very different footing from what it is at present and proper clergy placed at Quebec, Montreal and Three Rivers, even the name of the Church of England—all that exists of it at present—will in a few years be extirpated from Canada. . . ." *Ibid.*

[3] "At Quebec the only clergyman of the Church of England is a very

ferring to three clergymen who had come to Canada with the United Empire Loyalists spoke very highly of one, but described the other two as "miserably indigent, too ignorant and insignificant in every respect, to be the least dangerous." [1]

Bishop Inglis, during his visitation of the province became convinced that the policy of appointing foreign clergy to incumbencies had been disadvantageous to the interests of the church. In a letter to Dorchester, he writes that, "The introduction of so many foreign clergymen into Quebec was an ill-judged measure, and has had a very unhappy effect on our church. I had much conversation on the subject with the Archbishop of Canterbury; he lamented the case and mentioned the expedient which he had proposed to your Lordship as most eligible to obviate the evil." [2] He is probably more generous in his criticism of the clergymen whom he found in charge of the various parishes; yet he refers to the clergyman at Quebec, as a foreigner who "spoke very bad English—could scarcely be understood and although not deficient in abilities, nor chargeable with any immorality, yet his address and manners disqualified him for the station, and he seemed utterly unacquainted with the constitution, usages and regulations of our church." At the evening prayer he "read the service miserably and I could not understand half of his sermon." In summing up the situation at the time of his visit,

old Swedish gentleman, who cannot speak one word of unbroken English, and because of his unpopular private conduct the English inhabitants at Quebec—which are numerous and respectable—are deprived of Divine Service and the minister is an object of contempt and ridicule. At Montreal the case is the same. . . . At Three Rivers the situation is still more unfortunate, and may be justly called shameful." *Ibid.*, Q. 26, pt. i, p. 22.

[1] *Ibid.*, Q. 26, pt. i, p. 62.

[2] *C. A.*, M. 914, p. 94.

he writes, "there are only eight clergymen of the Church of England; of these three are foreigners and cannot speak English intelligently." [1]

The absence of proper oversight was responsible in part for this situation. Until the erection of the Episcopal See of Nova Scotia in 1787,[2] the Church of England, in Quebec, had been under the jurisdiction of the Bishop of London.[3] Early in the summer of 1789, Bishop Inglis made his first visitation of the province, and his report to the Archbishop of Canterbury the same year makes it clear that the congregations had been practically without organization.[4] Both Bishop Inglis, personally while in Quebec, and the British government through Lord Dorchester sought to remedy this weakness.[5] This unhappy state of the church of England, as revealed in Bishop Inglis's report, therefore made it apparent that if the dream of a national church was ever to be realized the church must have more adequate supervision and support. In 1793, four years later, the Protestant Bishopric of Quebec was erected and Dr. Mountain, an English clergy-

[1] *Ibid.*, M. 914, p. 154 *et seq.*

[2] *Ibid.*, Q. 28, p. 27.

[3] *Ibid.*, Q. 26b, p. 27.

[4] *C. A.*, M. 914, pp. 154, 206.

[5] "You are to take especial care that . . . the services and Prayers appointed by and according to the Book of Common Prayer be publicly and solemnly read and performed throughout the Year.

"You are to be careful that the Churches which are or may be hereafter erected in Our said Province of Lower Canada be well and orderly kept.

"You shall recommend to the Legislative Council and General Assemblies of the Province of Lower Canada to settle the Limits of Parishes in such a manner as shall be deemed most convenient.

"You are to use your best Endeavours that every Minister be constituted one of the Vestry in his respective Parish, and that no Vestry be held without him, except in case of his sickness, or that, after notice of a Vestry, he omit to come." (Instructions to Lord Dorchester, *Const. Docs.*, vol. ii, p. 26.)

man, was appointed bishop of the diocese. Bishop Mountain, unlike his predecessor the Bishop of Nova Scotia, was at a disadvantage in having had no colonial experience. Unaccustomed to the conditions in a new country, he was both confident and determined that the Church of England in Quebec, should occupy the place of authority and dignity which the national church did in England.

Unlike the situation in the American Colonies, there appears to have been little opposition on the part of any considerable number of nonconformists to the appointment of a resident bishop.[1] There is reason to believe, however, that the Roman Catholics were somewhat apprehensive.[2]

In addition to the facts that some of the clergy were unsuited for their tasks and that the church lacked adequate supervision, the Church of England was further handicapped in its race for ecclesiastical control in not having its own church buildings. It is true that the garrison at Quebec had the use of the *Récollet* church,[3] and that the members of the Church of England had the use of no less than three churches, two of which belonged to, and were used also by, the Roman Catholics.[4] Nevertheless it was equally true, as pointed out by the Reverend Mr. Toosey, in a letter to the Bishop of Lincoln, as well as by others, that there was not " a single church or chapel in Lower Canada belonging to the members of the Church of England; at Quebec, they

[1] Kingsford, *op. cit.*, vol. vii, p. 265 *et seq.;* Herbert L. Osgood, *The American Colonies in the Seventeenth Century*, vol. i, pp. 207-208, 294; vol. ii, p. 245, 331-333; vol. iii, pp. 390-391; Edward Channing, *A History of the United States*, vol. ii, pp. 429, 431-434.

[2] *C. A.*, Q. 83, p. 336.

[3] *C. A.*, M. 384, p. 60.

[4] ". . . Mr. Montmolin, notwithstanding we have in this town the use of two churches in common with the Roman Catholics and one entirely to ourselves." Carleton to Hillsborough, July 21, 1768, *C. A.*, Q. 5, pt. ii, p. 727.

assemble in a Popish chapel before or after the Popish service."[1] This plan of using the Roman Catholic churches at such times as they were not being used by their own members was very unsatisfactory; not only was "the shifting of pews, seats and books on every occasion" necessary, but the place of worship had to be moved "with the change of the seasons to different places all depending upon the precarious tenure and will of their neighbors and fellow citizens of the Roman Catholic persuasion."[2]

The inconvenience thus occasioned, added to the thought of the national church being dependent upon the hospitality of the Roman Catholics, was considered by many to be most humiliating.[3] The Archbishop of Canterbury wrote to the Duke of Portland pointing out what he called "the mortifying and degrading state of the Church of England in the Province of Quebec for want of the convenience of a decent place of divine worship even in the capital."[4] As the Protestant population increased, they became emphatic in their demands for an adequate church establishment.[5] It was claimed that their church was not getting the support from the government that they had been led to expect; in fact, the time had long passed when their expectations should have been fulfilled.[6]

At first, they desired to have the government hand over one of the numerous Roman Catholic churches. They maintained that Quebec with a population of 7,000, of which

[1] *C. A.*, Q. 66, p. 271; *cf.* Q. 43, pt. ii, p. 606.

[2] *A Memorial and Petition of the Members of the Church of England to Guy Lord Dorchester*, 1789, *C. A.*, Q. 43, pt. ii, p. 607; *cf. C. A.*, M. 914, p. 154.

[3] *C. A.*, M. 914, p. 154.

[4] *C. A.*, Q. 79, pt. ii, p. 453.

[5] Dartmouth Papers, *C. A.*, M. 384, vol. ii, p. 99.

[6] *C. A.*, Q. 83, p. 332 *et seq.*; *cf. C. A.*, Q. 43, pt. ii, p. 606.

about one-fifth was Protestant, had ten Roman Catholic churches and they could well spare one.[1] In Montreal, the same year, a similar request was made asking the government "to order the grant of the said church [Jesuit] and also a small piece of ground adjacent thereto for the purpose of building a vestry room."[2]

After the destruction by fire of the *Récollet* church, at Quebec, the Roman Catholic bishop offered the use of the Jesuit chapel to the Protestants.[3] This building was used for a time, but was soon considered inadequate to the needs of the Anglican communion. By the year 1796 this feeling had become so strong that it was urged to be "not an unfavorable moment for asking His Majesty's gracious protection and support for the Church of England—that its members may obtain . . . a decent, suitable and independent Place of Divine Worship."[4] This matter was referred to the home government and strongly supported by the Archbishop of Canterbury.[5] Finally, the sanction of the government was obtained for the erection of a place of worship and for the transfer of the old site of the *Récollet* church to the Church of England.[6] The building of a metropolitan church was soon undertaken, and carried to completion by funds provided, in large part, from the public treasury.[7]

[1] *C. A.*, Q. 43, pt. ii, p. 609; *cf.* Dartmouth Papers, *C. A.*, M. 384, p. 60.

[2] *C. A.*, Q. 43, pt. ii, p. 612 *et seq.*

[3] *Ibid.*, Q. 77, pp. 216-217.

[4] *Ibid.*, Q. 79, pt. ii, p. 455.

[5] *Ibid.*, p. 453.

[6] *C. A.*, Q. 82, p. 288 *et seq.; cf. ibid.*, Q. 89, p. 102.

[7] *C. A.*, Q. 84, p. 4; *ibid.*, Q. 86, pt. i, p. 10. "From representation made to you by the commissioners for erecting the Metropolitan Church in Quebec, your compliance with their request for the advance of necessary sums to enable them to proceed without interruption in completing the building was certainly proper. . . ." Instructions to Sir Robert Shore Milnes, *C. A.*, Q. 89, p. 96; *cf.* also *ibid.*, Q. 88, pp. 151-152.

One of the most important tasks confronting the Church of England was to secure an adequate revenue for the support of the increased establishment. For although the Quebec Act had reserved to the Crown the "accustomed Dues and Rights" for the encouragement of the Protestant religion,[1] and the Constitutional Act had provided for the "Allotment and Appropriation" of government lands,[2] no definite scheme had been worked out for giving practical effect to these provisions.[3]

Apart from some help from the Society for the Propagation of the Gospel, three sources of revenue seemed open, namely: voluntary offerings, tithes, and state grants of money and lands.

The voluntary offerings of the people, from which the government had expected much, proved disappointing. These could not be estimated usually at more than forty or fifty pounds sterling.[4] Portland, in a dispatch of the 22nd of June 1796, wrote to Dorchester, "I cannot omit this opportunity of reminding your Lordship of the propriety of keeping alive the attention of the Colonists in your Government to the idea of making a suitable provision for their own Clergy."[5] It was further urged that "the King's Bounty" was not intended to relieve the people of their financial obligations to the church.[6] In order to encourage the people to assume some responsibility for the support of the clergy, the establishment of rectories was made to depend largely upon the disposition of the parishioners to contribute. The insistence of the officials, however, that

[1] Imperial Act, 14 Geo. III, cap. lxxxiii, *Const. Docs.*, vol. i, p. 403.

[2] Imp. Act, 31 Geo. III, cap. xxxi, *ibid.*, p. 704.

[3] *C. A.*, Q. 69, pt. ii, p. 368 *et seq.*

[4] *Ibid.*, Q. 83, p. 390.

[5] *Ibid.*, Q. 75, pt. ii, p. 265.

[6] *Ibid.*, Q. 86, pt. i, p. 10.

the subscriptions of parishioners should be guaranteed on the security of their land, proved a failure as it was strongly opposed by both the settlers [1] and the Colonial Office.[2]

The question as to whether the Constitutional Act had conferred authority upon the Protestant churches to collect tithes from Protestants, remained for a time open to dispute. At first, the Colonial Office seemed to favor the interpretation of the Church of England, that the Act did confer this right, in Canada. In a letter to the Bishop of Quebec, of November 14, 1794, Portland makes this very clear, for he states, "there cannot be a shadow of a doubt relative to the construction of the late Canada Act which annexes to Rectories and Parsonages erected under the same the enjoyment of all the Rights, Profits and Emoluments, belonging to a Parsonage or Rectory in England which must necessarily include tythes, . . . "[3] The following year, in a dispatch to Dorchester, he expressed the same opinion, "I should apprehend tythes are comprehended in the general terms therein used, and which give to Rectories and Parsonages erected under the same, the enjoyment of all Rights, Profits and Emoluments belonging to a Parsonage or Rectory in England."[4]

It remained for the attorney general, Sewell, the same year, to point out that while the incumbent of a Protestant parish, by law, could enjoy the rights belonging to his rectory in the same manner as an incumbent could in England, nevertheless this did not entitle him to tithes, for this right had never been granted, by the Crown, to the Protestant clergy in Canada.[5] Similarly, the opinion had been ex-

[1] *C. A.*, Q. 83, pp. 225, 390.

[2] *Ibid.*, 82, p. 295.

[3] *Ibid.*, 69, pt. ii, p. 400.

[4] *Ibid.*, 71, pt. i, p. 92.

[5] *Const. Docs.*, vol. ii, pp. 191-193.

pressed with regard to the authority of a rector, church wardens, and vestry, to call a parish meeting for the purpose of assessing the people,—which had been attempted in the borough of William Henry,—that there was no statute or act from which such a right could be derived.[1] These opinions, if upheld, Bishop Mountain saw would greatly weaken the status of the Protestant establishment, and he at once urged upon Lord Dorchester "the necessity of legislative interference for the better regulation of ecclesiastical affairs." [2]

Dorchester's dispatch of October 10, 1795, to Portland, enclosing a number of documents, revealed a wide difference of opinion, in the province, with respect to tithes. One of these, from the minister, wardens, vestry and congregation of Christ Church, Montreal, was in the form of a petition, praying that, "Letters Patent might be used erecting the said church into a parsonage, endowing the rector, wardens and vestry with corporate powers conformably to the statute of Geo. III, chap. 31, but without subjecting the parishioners by such establishment to the payment either of tythes or parish rates." [3] This petition showed there was opposition to tithes even within the Anglican communion.

The Colonial Office now saw, both from the standpoint of law and of public policy, that some other means had to be devised for the maintenance of religious ordinances until such time as the church lands should produce sufficient revenue.[4] In Portland's dispatch of July, 1799, the changed attitude is clearly shown. The incumbent of a parish, he writes, has no right to tithes, and "no such right can exist except by special grant from His Majesty." [5]

[1] *Const. Docs.*, vol. ii, pp. 189, 190.

[2] *C. A.*, Q. 74, pt. ii, p. 207.

[3] *Ibid.*, pt. i, p. 199.

[4] *C. A.*, Q. 75, pt. ii, p. 265.

[5] *Ibid.*, Q. 82, p. 291.

According to the Quebec Act of 1774, he further points out that while the Roman Catholic clergy were entitled to receive their ancient rights and dues, this did not exempt the Protestants from obligation to pay tithes, since the Act provided that,

it should be lawful for His Majesty to make provision out of the rest of the said accustomed dues and rights for the maintenance and support of a Protestant Clergy.

Neither did it give any right to a Protestant Clergyman to exact tythes even from Protestants, the right of collecting them was wholly vested in the King, who might relax or enforce that right, as might be judged expedient.[1]

The same held true of the Constitutional Act, which declared that "every person presented to a Parsonage or Rectory shall hold the same and all rights, profits and emoluments thereunto belonging or granted as fully and amply and in the same manner, *etc.*, as the incumbent of a rectory or parsonage in England," but which, however, did not determine what rights belonged to clergymen in Canada, much less include the taking of tithes. This was the prerogative of the king and had never been granted to the Protestant clergy.[2]

The foundation of the Protestant establishment in Canada, however, was not intended to rest on voluntary offerings or tithes, but on the lands which should be set apart, in every new settlement, as clergy reserves. These were to consist of one-seventh of all the land thrown open for settlement, and were to be selected in such a way as to be most likely to share in the unearned increment, or as the

[1] *Ibid.*, p. 292; *cf.* also Imp. Act, 14 Geo. III, cap. lxxxiii, *Const. Docs.*, vol. i, p. 403.

[2] *Ibid.*, Q. 82, p. 293; *cf.* Imp. Act, 31 Geo. III, cap. xxxi, *Const. Docs.*, vol. i, pp. 703-704.

act stated, "between the other farms of which the said township shall consist."[1] This large proportion of the land in each settlement, it was considered would soon provide an adequate revenue for the maintenance of the new establishment and render unnecessary the taking of tithes or the placing of any undue burden upon the parishioners.[2]

In the meantime the Colonial Office supplemented the stipends of the clergy from the provincial revenues. Except in very special cases the allowance did not exceed £100 sterling for each clergyman.[3] The grant was looked upon only as a temporary expedient by the Crown and it was repeatedly suggested to the legislature to "devise some mode of making a provision for its officiating clergy."[4]

The foregoing discussion of the establishment of the Church of England reveals how inadequate were its resources to cope with the tremendous task of assimilation assigned to it by the government. Even for ministering to the religious needs of its own small constituency its resources in organization, leadership and material support compared very unfavorably with those of its well organized and strongly entrenched rival, the Roman Catholic church. This being the case it was not to be expected that the Church of England could accomplish much either in Angli-

[1] *Const. Docs.*, vol. ii, p. 61.

[2] *C. A.*, Q. 71, pt. i, p. 93; *cf.* also *ibid.*, Q. 75, pt. ii, p. 265.

[3] ". . . you will consider yourself authorized to make a temporary addition to such allowance from the Provincial Revenues of an annual sum not exceeding 100 pounds, except in very particular cases where the nature and consequence of the situation and of its duties may call for it, to be continued to such incumbent until some Act of the Legislature, or the improvement of the Church Revenues, shall afford the means of securing to him an adequate provision, without having recourse to the means above mentioned." *C. A.*, Q. 82, p. 295; *cf.* also *ibid.*, Q. 83, p. 390.

[4] *C. A.*, Q. 82, p. 294.

cizing the French Canadian population or in weakening the control of the Roman Catholic church.

In fact the opposite was true. The attempt to establish the Church of England as the national church and to extend state support to the sister Church of Scotland necessarily advanced the interests of the Roman Catholic church.[1]

The Protestant Bishopric of Quebec entitled the bishop to membership in the Legislative Council with the title of Lord Bishop of Quebec. This honor was claimed, at once, by Bishop Mountain on his arrival in the province,[2] for both the bishop and many members of the Anglican communion considered it of the first importance that the head of the church should have a seat in parliament as in England. There was some question whether as a member of the Privy or Legislative Councils he would be able to render the larger service to the church. Finally, however, he was appointed to the Legislative Council,[3] although without salary,[4] as it was considered that as a legislator he would guard the church's interests more carefully and perfect its establishment.[5] The privileges sought by the Protestant churches could hardly be withheld from the Roman

[1] *C. A.*, Q. 28, p. 165; *cf. ibid.*, Q. 89, p. 21.

[2] "By His Majesty's ship Severn which sailed on the 6th, I had the honor to inform you that we arrived at Quebec on the 1st of this month; having taken an early opportunity of presenting my patent to Lord Dorchester, I learnt upon that occasion with the utmost surprize that His Majesty's mandamus constituting the Bishop of this Diocese a member of the Legislative Council with the title of Lord Bishop of Quebec had not come to his Lordship's hands. . . ." *C. A.*, Q. 69, pt. ii, p. 381.

[3] "The Bishop has sent me two mandamus writs for his being styled Lord Bishop of Upper and Lower Canada and called to the Legislative Council of both provinces: patents will be prepared accordingly." *C. A.*, Q. 71, pt. i, p. 6; *cf.* also *ibid.*, Q. 83, p. 356.

[4] *C. A.*, Q. 77, p. 358; *cf.* also *ibid.*, Q. 79, pt. ii, p. 430.

[5] *C. A.*, Q. 69, pt. ii, pp. 368-369.

Catholic church which represented such a large proportion of the population.[1] This was soon recognized by Dorchester.[2] In a letter to Portland, of December 1795, giving a list of the names of those recommended for appointment to the Legislative Council, he writes,

The name of the Reverend Jean Francois Hubert, our Roman Catholic Bishop is omitted in the list of those recommended, as this measure may seem to deserve a more particular consideration, but for my part, seeing it has been thought advisable to give our Protestant Bishop a political character in this province where his proportion in the cure of souls is that of seventy in two thousand, I cannot but recommend that the same honor be conferred on Mr. Hubert, who has always shown himself a very good subject much retired from the world, and somewhat devout.[3]

It may readily be seen from this attitude of Dorchester that he considered the rights and privileges granted to the Church of England could hardly be withheld from the Roman Catholic church. This was soon recognized by the Anglican Bishop for in writing to Portland, with regard to the anticipation of the Protestants and the apprehension of the Roman Catholics, at the appointment of a Protestant bishop, he further remarks: "But both parties have long been undeceived. The Catholics, elevated to a higher degree of security and confidence than before, look down with contempt upon the fruitless efforts that have been made to raise the Church of England to a competent degree of independence and respect. They well knew that the political

[1] *C. A.*, Q. 75, pt. i, p. 48 *et seq.*

[2] Dorchester to Dundas, *C. A.*, Q. 71, pt. i, p. 5; *cf. C. A.*, Q. 68, pp. 132-133.

[3] Dorchester to Portland, *C. A.*, Q. 75, pt. i, p. 48.

influence of their prelate, however silent and unobtrusive in its operation, infinitely outweighs his." [1]

The Constitutional Act in dividing the Province of Quebec into the two provinces of Upper and Lower Canada,[2] left the population of Lower Canada overwhelmingly French and Roman Catholic.[3] It is true that there had been considerable immigration of English-speaking Protestants into what was now Lower Canada; but these were relatively few compared with their numerous French Canadian neighbors. The hierarchy soon seems to have realized that the English must always remain numerically inferior. Bishop Hubert, in a letter to Cardinal Antonelli at Rome, makes it clear that he felt no alarm at the volume of English immigration then coming to Quebec for he writes,

This colony which is naturally fertile, is being considerably extended from day to day not only by the settlements made by the English, but also by those made by the Canadians. The dominant religion is still the Roman Catholic, and, although during the twenty-nine years which have passed since England conquered us a large number of English Protestants have come to Canada, they are, however, and will probably always remain much less numerous than the Roman Catholics; so much so that in, (at least) a third of the country parishes, it would be difficult to find three Protestant families. . . . I have observed on my pastoral visitations the firm faith and attachment of our people to our Holy Religion. . . . [4]

This firm faith and attachment among such a large proportion of the population made it easy for the church to remain dominant in ecclesiastical affairs.

[1] *C. A.*, Q. 83, pp. 334, 336, 337.

[2] *Const. Docs.*, vol. i, p. 695.

[3] *C. A.*, Q. 75, pt. i, p. 48.

[4] *C. A.*, M. 128, p. 347.

The Constitutional Act of 1791 marked the culmination of the development of the system of ecclesiastical control. Through the extension of self-government which gave the franchise to the French Canadians there was opened to the church the further avenue to power through its influence at the polls.[1]

With the granting of the Constitutional Act the legal status of the Roman Catholic church in Quebec was assured, and ecclesiastical control was achieved. Few changes of fundamental importance for the Roman Catholic church have been made since its passage. The subsequent development of ecclesiastical control in Quebec is but the outgrowth of the privileges and prerogative accorded to it by the British government before the end of the eighteenth century.

[1] *Const. Docs.*, vol. i, p. 697 *et seq.*

CHAPTER VI

Summary and Conclusion

The purpose of this study as set forth in the Introduction was to indicate from a sociological point of view the close relation of the rise of ecclesiastical control and the social solidarity upon which it was based, to the great demographic and social facts of the Province of Quebec. The study has sought to review the facts which show how inevitably the population became homogeneous, and how for this reason there developed a social solidarity which was highly favorable to the development of a centralized and paternalistic ecclesiastical control.

The demographic and social conditions were dealt with in Part I chapters II and III. In chapter II, these underlying demographic factors which affected the homogeneity of the population of Quebec were dealt with under the headings of situation, aggregation, demotic composition and demotic unity. The situation, in its natural features, in its artificial features and in the sources of subsistence was shown to have been remarkably conducive to homogeneity of population. This was seen to have been brought about by the system of waterways which provided an easy means of access to the newer districts and by the seigniorial system of land tenure which tended to produce many scattered communities of essentially the same type. Within the local settlements, further, the relatively dense population along the river banks afforded unusual opportunities for inter-communication among the inhabitants and gradually developed a high degree of mental unity.

Thus, because the territory was settled by a single population type, namely that of the Roman Catholic French, each small community soon became composed of persons relatively alike in descent, language and religion. Inasmuch as the river and seigniorial systems led to the founding of many such local groups, at about the same time and by the same population type there resulted a remarkable similarity among the local groups. The relative isolation of these different settlements in the early days of the colony which had permitted relatively little inter-communication among the various communities, nevertheless laid the foundation for homogeneity and subsequent social solidarity for the entire province. When later a well developed system of communication by roads was added to the increasing use of the rivers, the inter-relationships established readily produced a mental and moral solidarity throughout the whole territory.

The privations and hardships incident to pioneer life in a new country also operated to create a single homogeneous type of population. Natural resources were abundant but not such as to create great differences in wealth between the successful and unsuccessful. The exploitation of these resources required much severe toil. In consequence, only the vigorous could remain permanently on the land. The process of selection of necessity gradually produced a remarkably homogeneous type of population, thrifty and self-satisfied, traditionalistic and conservative in the extreme.

The population, furthermore, was essentially homogeneous in its descent. It is true the Indians were always a factor to be considered in shaping the policies of church and state; nevertheless as they never became an integral part of the local community, the element of heterogeneity which their presence introduced was never of great importance in relation to ecclesiastical control. The homogeneity and consequent social solidarity of the white population was merely intensified by the relations which grew out of the presence of the Indians.

From an ethnic and religious point of view the early white population of Quebec was highly homogeneous, for it was drawn almost altogether from France. Immigration, which had been stimulated by active organization in France before 1680, began to show a marked decline so that the French Canadian population rapidly became a genetic aggregation, that is, a population produced by natural increase rather than by migration.

The demotic composition of Quebec was relatively uniform, for immigration had been drawn from all parts of France. The different racial elements of the French population, found a common area of assimilation so that the ethnographical diversities gradually disappeared through amalgamation in Quebec.

This amalgamation was further expedited by the widespread distribution of the immigrants on their arrival in the colony, by assisted immigration of girls and women of marriageable age, by the absence of any impediment to marriage on account of religious differences, by the decline of the *noblesse* and the leveling of classes. These facts, coupled with the encouragement given by the government to early marriages and large families, made the French Canadian population at the end of our period in 1791, a more homogeneous aggregation than even the population of France.

In chapter III, entitled Social and Moral Solidarity, the facts of occupation, language, religion and other social characteristics of the population were so treated as to indicate their relation to the same fundamental social condition, namely, mental and moral solidarity.

Occupation was not greatly diversified. Agriculture from a very small beginning steadily gained in importance until it was the leading industry. With the decline of the fur trade after the conquest and the passing of general trading more and more into the hands of the British, the proportion of French Canadians engaged in agriculture steadily increased until at the end of our period (1791) it is most probable that eighty per cent of the French Canadians were living in the open country or in small rural villages and that they possessed all the traditionalism and conservatism peculiar to a homogeneous agricultural population.

Uniformity of language further intensified the social solidarity resulting from uniformity of occupation. At the conquest French was practically the only language spoken. The fusion of the early settlers among whom the French-speaking predominated, had been so complete, that, in a comparatively short time the French language had received universal acceptance. The attempt of the British after the conquest to introduce English met with strong opposition from the Roman Catholic hierarchy and ended in failure.

In this way the French language, in the hands of the church became an effective weapon of isolation, warding off modernism in every form. For, on the one hand, English ideas were successfully shut out, and on the other, all French literature was so carefully censored that only those French ideas which were in complete harmony with the church were allowed to get in. The barrier of language thus became another stepping stone in the rise of ecclesiastical control. Uniformity of language, however, was shown to have been only one of the factors which, by intensifying social solidarity, made ecclesiastical control easy.

The absence of interests and organizations other than the church rendered the foregoing influences peculiarly potent in creating similarity of thought and custom. The state discouraged its citizens from having any voice in directing public affairs and the church jealously guarded its social and religious leadership in the parishes. The *coureurs de bois,* unwilling to withstand repressive policies, sought the freedom of the interior, and so rendered the carrying-out of unifying policies among the settled population less difficult. The pressure of pioneer life in the parishes left little opportunity for developing new interests among the *habitants.* The absence of other interests undoubtedly accounted in large part for the important place which the church occupied in the life of the French Canadians.

The vast majority of the people, as was pointed out, were subjected to relatively simple stimuli both in the process of exploiting their environment and in the expression of their social, political and religious life through the activities of the parish church. In this way the continued like-response to the common stimuli was most important in developing social solidarity.

The characteristics of the French Canadians also made them readily subject to ecclesiastical control during this period. The prevailing type of character although forceful and convivial was devoutly religious. Ideo-emotional in type of mind, they were swayed largely by feeling. Reason had little opportunity to assert itself. They clung to their ancient laws and customs, not because of the realized value of these laws and customs, but because of their traditionalistic and conservative type of mind. Such traits likewise rendered them readily amenable to the unquestioned authority of the church.

It was in the sphere of religion, however, that even a greater degree of homogeneity was exhibited. The strict exclusion of Protestants had been of primary importance for the unity of faith and practise. Everywhere throughout New France there was uniformity of worship. There was one church and one religious leadership, under the supervision of a watchful bishop. The attendance at church represented the whole community. The presence of a strong large body of clergy in the colony, backed by a highly organized church with liberal financial support, and in control of education, gave to the church in Quebec, stability and prestige in the older parishes, and enabled it to do effective home mission work in the newer settlements. It is not surprising therefore that the church, thus strongly organized and adequately supported, unchallenged by any rival, religious or otherwise, except the state, should have been able to strengthen its influence and to centralize its control. The possession of this immense centralized control, as has been shown, not only brought the church into conflict with the state but of necessity tended to a zealous guardianship of the control itself on the part of the church authorities.

Thus in considering the sociological basis for explaining the evolution of ecclesiastical control, the facts of situation, natural resources, population, occupation, language, social organization, psychological characteristics of the inhabitants, religious and educational institutions all were shown to have been conducive to the production of the remarkably homogeneous population and a well developed mental and moral solidarity.

The evolution of ecclesiastical control itself was dealt with in part II, chapters IV and V, from an historical standpoint.

Chapter IV traced the evolution of ecclesiastical control in the French period, and dealt with the forces both favorable and unfavorable to the rise and development of this control. Among the more favorable forces were the interest of the explorers and colonizers in the conversion of the natives, the devotion of the early missionaries, the political influence of the Jesuits, the services rendered by the missionaries to the state in its relation to the Indians, and the establishment of the Archbishopric of Quebec independent of the Gallican Church and directly subject to the See of Rome. The unfavorable forces were shown to be the increased emphasis placed by Colbert and succeeding administrations on the economic interests of the colony and the assertion of the king's supremacy in all temporal matters. This changed attitude was shown in the opposition of the Sovereign Council to the domination of the Roman Catholic hierarchy, as well as in the active interference by the state respecting tithes, religious houses, the public ministry of the church and other clerical encroachments. In this way the state, from being the servant of the church, gradually became supreme. The theocratic influences which had predominated from the beginning of ecclesiastical control under the Jesuits gave way before the progressive colonial policy of Louis XIV and his ministers. From that time to the end of French rule, except for the brief term of Denonville after the recall of Frontenac, the temporal influence of the church in Quebec steadily declined.

Thus it is probable that the Roman Catholic church in Quebec would never have gained its position of power and authority had it not been for the British conquest. The defeat of the French on the Plains of Abraham was a victory for Roman Catholicism in Quebec. The statement that the church might profit by a "change of masters" soon proved to be true, notwithstanding the desire of the British government to have it otherwise.

Chapter V reviewed the details of the relation of Church and State under British rule up to 1791. During this period the existing social solidarity was shown to be of fundamental importance for the development of ecclesiastical control, because many of the British government's attempts to adjust its policies to that solidarity, necessarily reacted to increase the power of the church.

The friction created by the attempt to assimilate the French Canadian population through the introduction of English law, greatly strengthened the Roman Catholic clergy in that it made them the leaders of the people against the policies of their conquerors. In this way the clergy became the logical and actual, though not the legal, successors of the French civil authorities who had returned to France. Among the other important factors noted as strengthening the control of the church were: the concessions which the British government considered it wise to make in order to retain the loyalty of this homogeneous population; and the loyalty of the Roman Catholic hierarchy to the British government during the Revolutionary War. The inevitable outcome of the attempt to establish the Church of England was shown to have been an increase in the power of the Roman Catholic church. The separation of the Province of Quebec into Upper and Lower Canada in 1791 was a further adjustment to the social solidarity of the French Canadians. By thus separating the two races and at the same time extending the franchise to them, the political control of Lower Canada was secured to the French Canadians. It was inevitable therefore, in view of the powerful position of leadership occupied by the clergy, that the political and social control of the Roman Catholic church should have the supreme position it now holds.

The rise of ecclesiastical control in Quebec is seen, therefore, to have been the outcome of many peculiar social conditions as well as a result of conditions generally classed as specifically political. The demographic factors of Quebec tended to develop a highly homogeneous population. This homogeneity brought about a remarkable social and moral solidarity which reacted very favorably to the rise of ecclesiastical control. The despotic power of the state under French rule, however, was able partly to offset the influence of this social and moral solidarity and to bring about a decline in the temporal authority of the church. After the conquest, however, the attempt of the British government to assimilate the French Canadians intensified this solidarity by uniting the clergy and people in a common struggle to retain their laws and to defend their religion. Finally, the concessions which this alliance of the clergy and people obtained from the British government through the Constitutional Act and previous legislation, secured to the Roman Catholic church in Quebec those constitutional rights which have made it possible for the church to mould the homogeneous French Canadian population to its purpose. It was through the operation of these forces that the Roman Catholic church in Quebec rose to its present position of unparalleled ecclesiastical control.

BIBLIOGRAPHY

I. Manuscript Sources

	Abbreviations used for works cited more than once.
Canadian Archives.	
Original Collections:	
Series G. Original despatches to governors and lieutenant-governors from the Colonial Office.	*C. A.*, G.
Transcripts from England:	
Series Q. Original papers at the Public Record Office, composed of the correspondence of the governors, lieutenant-governors, and administrators of Quebec (Lower Canada) and Upper Canada from the first years of British rule to 1841.	*C. A.*, Q.
Series B. Haldimand Papers in the British Museum, including the correspondence of Frederick Haldimand, and a large part of Sir Guy Carleton's public papers.	*C. A.*, B. Haldimand Papers.
Transcripts from France:	
Series B. Registers, letters and books, in which were dispatches, memoranda and other papers sent out by the French king and the minister to the officials, ecclesiastics and other persons in the colony.	*C. A.*, B.
Series C[11]. *Correspondance Génèrale du Canada*, official and miscellaneous correspondence and other papers received from Canada. It is thus complementary to Series B.	*C. A.*, C[11].
Series F[2]. Papers and correspondence dealing with missions and religious worship, 1658-1782.	*C. A.*, F[2].

Series F³. *Moreau de St. Méry.* A collection of papers especially valuable in showing the paternalism of the French government. — *C. A.*, F³.

Series G. Registers, land records, and census statistics, including the general censuses of Canada from 1685-1739.

English Archives.

British Museum:

The King's Manuscripts.

French Archives.

Bibliothèque Nationale:

Fonds Français.

Nouvelles Acquisitions Françaises. — *Nouv. Acq. Fr.*

II. Contemporary Published Sources

Annual Register. London, 1758-1811, 54 vols.

Baxter, J. P. *A Memoir of Jacques Cartier.* New York, 1906.

Brymner, Douglas. *Reports on Canadian Archives.* Ottawa, 1872-1903.

Cavendish, Sir Henry. *Debates of the House of Commons in the year 1774, on the Bill for making more effectual provision for the government of the Province of Quebec.* London, 1839. — Cavendish.

Census of Canada 1870-1871. Vol. iv, Census Report of New France and Lower Canada. — *Census.*

Champeaux, Gilbert de. *Le droit civil ecclésiastique français, ancien et moderne dans ses rapports avec le droit canon et la législation actuelle.* Paris, 1848, 2 vols. — Champeaux.

Champlain. *Les voyages de la Nouvelle-France Occidentale,* 1603-1629. Paris, 1632.

———. *Œuvres de Champlain. Par* C. H. Laverdière. Québec, 1870, 6 vols.

———. *Voyages of Samuel de Champlain. Publications of the Prince Society.* Boston, 1880, 3 vols.

Charlevoix, P. F. X. *Histoire et description générale de la Nouvelle-France.* Paris, 1744. Trans. by J. G. Shea, New York, 1866. 6 vols. — Charlevoix.

Collection de manuscrits contenant lettres, mémoires, et autres documents historiques relatifs à la Nouvelle-France. Québec, 1883-1885, 4 vols.

Constitutional Documents. *Documents relating to the Constitutional History of Canada*, 1759-1791. Ed. with notes by Adam Shortt and A. G. Doughty. Ottawa, 1907. — *Const. Docs.*

Constitutional Documents. *Documents relating to the Constitutional History of Canada*, 1791-1818. Ed. with notes by A. G. Doughty and Duncan MacArthur. Ottawa, 1914. — *Const. Docs.*

Doughty, A. G. *Reports on Canadian Archives.* Ottawa, 1904-1914.

Edicts and Ordinances. An Abstract of the royal edicts and declarations and provincial regulations and ordinances that were in force in the Province of Quebec in the time of the French Government, collected from the registers of the Superior Council. London, 1772.

Edits, Ordonnances Royaux, Déclarations, et Arrêts de Conseil de d'Etat du Roi concernant le Canada. Québec, 1803-1806, 2 vols. New ed., 1854-1856, 3 vols. — *Edits et Ord.*

Extract of the Proceedings of a Committee of the Whole Council Regarding Changing Land Tenure. Quebec, 1790.

Gee and Hardy. *Documents Illustrative of English Church History.* London, 1906.

Jesuit Relations and Allied Documents. Thwaites ed. Cleveland, 1894, 73 vols. — *Rel.*

Jugements et délibérations du Conseil Souverain de la Nouvelle-France. Québec, 1885, 4 vols. — *Jugements et Dél.*

Kalm, Peter. *Travels in North America.* London, 1771, 3 vols. — Kalm.

La Hontan, Baron de. *Nouveaux Voyages.* The Hague, 1705, 2 vols. Pinkerton ed., London, 1812. Thwaites ed., Chicago, 1905, 2 vols. — La Hontan.

Lescarbot, Marc. *Histoire de la Nouvelle-France.* English translation by Grant and Biggar, *Publications of the Champlain Society. Toronto*, 1907, 3 vols. — Lescarbot.

Mandements, lettres pastorales, et circulaires, des evêques de Québec. Publiés par Têtu, et Gagnon. Quebec, 1887-1897, 6 vols. — *Mandements.*

Margry, Pierre. *Mémoires et documents pour servir à l'histoire des origines françaises des pays d'outremer.* Paris, 1876-1886, 6 vols.

Masères, Francis. *The Canadian Freeholder.* London, 1776, 3 vols.

———. *An Account of the Proceedings of the British and Other Protestant Inhabitants of the Province of Quebec, in North America, in order to obtain an House of Assembly in that Province.* London, 1775, 2 vols. — Masères.

Munro, W. B. *Documents Relating to Seigniorial Tenure in Canada 1598-1854.* Toronto, 1908. — Munro, *Docs. S. T.*

Ordinances Made for the Province of Quebec by the Governor and Council. Quebec, 1767.

Review of Government, and Grievances of the Province of Quebec since the Conquest. London, 1788.

Richard, Edouard. *Supplement to Dr. Brymner's Report on Canadian Archives.* Ottawa, 1901.

Rochemonteix, P. C. de. *Les Jésuites et la Nouvelle-France.* Paris, 1895-1896, 3 vols.

Sagard, Gabriel. *Le grand voyage du pays des Hurons.* Paris, 1632.

Saint-Valier, Jean. *Etat présent de l'Église et de la colonie française dans la Nouvelle-France.* Paris, 1688; Québec, 1856.

Stone, and Hund. *Letters of Brunswick and Hessian Officers during the American Revolution.* Albany, 1891. — *Revolutionary Letters.*

Weld, Isaac. *Travels . . . Upper and Lower Canada during 1795, 1796 and 1797.* London, 1799, 2 vols.

III. Modern Published Sources

Bagwell, Richard. *Ireland under the Stuarts and during the Interregnum.* London, 1909, ... 2 vols.

Blackmar and Gillen. *Outlines of Sociology.* New York, 1915.

Bouchette, Joseph. *Topographical Description of the Province of Lower Canada.* London, 1815. — Bouchette.

Bourinot, Sir John G. *Canada under British Rule.* Cambridge, 1900.

Brasseur de Bourbourg. *Histoire du Canada, de son église et de ses missions, depuis la découverte de l'Amérique jusqu'à nos jours, écrite sur des documents inédits.* Paris, 1852, 2 vols.

Brumath, A. L. de. *Bishop Laval.* Toronto, 1906. Brumath.

Cahall, Raymond. *The Sovereign Council of New France.* New York, 1915. Cahall.

Canada and its Provinces: A History of the Canadian People and their Institutions by One Hundred Associates. Toronto, 1914, 22 vols.

Cambridge Modern History. New York, 1908, 14 vols.

Channing, Edward. *A History of the United States.* New York, 1905-1912, 3 vols.

Chapin, F. S. *An Introduction to the Study of Social Evolution.* New York, 1913.

Cooley, C. H. *Social Organization.* New York, 1909.

De Salles, Latteriére [ascribed to]. *A Political and Historical Account of Lower Canada.* London, 1830. *A Pol. and Hist. Account of L. C.*

Dionne, N. E. *Les Canadiens-Français: origine des familles.* Québec, 1914.

———. *Champlain.* London, 1905.

Durham, Earl of. *The Report of the Earl of Durham.* New York, 1902. Durham.

Duruy, Victor. *A History of France.*. New York, (1896).

Eastman, Mack. *Church and State in Early Canada.* Edinburgh, 1915.

Egerton, H. E. *A Short History of British Colonial Policy.* London, 1897.

Egerton and Grant. *Canadian Constitutional Development.* London, 1907.

Faillon, M. E. *Histoire de la colonie française en Canada.* Paris, 1865, 3 vols. Faillon.

Ferland, J. B. A. *Cours d'histoire du Canada.* Québec, 1865, 2 vols. Ferland.

Fiske, John. *New France and New England.* London, 1902.

Forsyth, William. *Constitutional Law.* London, 1869.

Garneau, F. X. *Histoire du Canada depuis sa découverte jusqu'à nos jours.* Montréal, 1882, 3 vols. Garneau.

Gérin, Léon. *Deux familles rurales* (in Royal Society of Canada, 1908). Ottawa.

Giddings, Franklin H. *Historical and Descriptive Sociology.* New York, 1909.

———. *Inductive Sociology.* New York, 1901.

——. "What Shall We Be." The Century Magazine, vol. lxv. New York, 1902-1903.

Gosselin, Auguste. *Vie de Mgr. Laval, premier évêque de Québec et apôtre du Canada.* Québec, 1890-1891.

———. *Les Normands au Canada.* Evreux, 1900.

———. *Henri de Bernières.* Québec, 1902.

———. *Le clergé Canadien et la déclaration de 1732* (in Royal Society Transactions, vol. vi, sec. i, 2d series). Ottawa, 1901.

Gosselin, Amédée E. *L'Instruction au Canada sous le régime français.* Québec, 1911. — Gosselin.

Jervis, W. H. P. *History of the Church of France.* London, 1872, 2 vols.

Johnson, A. H. *The Normans in Europe.* New York, 1888.

Kingsford, William. *The History of Canada.* Toronto, 1887-1898, 10 vols. — Kingsford.

La Tour, L'Abbé. *Vie de Mgr. Laval, premier évêque de Québec.* Cologne, 1760.

Le Sueur, W. D. *Count Frontenac.* Toronto, 1906.

Loreau, Edmond. *Histoire du droit Canadien.* Montréal, 1888, 2 vols.

Lorin, Henri. *Comte de Frontenac — étude sur le Canada Français à la fin du xvii siècle.* Paris, 1895.

Moeller, Wilhelm. *History of the Christian Church.* New York, 1900, 3 vols.

Moreau, M. *Histoire de l'Acadie Française de 1598 à 1755.* Paris, 1873.

Munro, W. B. *Seigniorial System in Canada.* New York, 1907.

Osgood, Herbert L. *The American Colonies in the Seventeenth Century.* New York, 1904, 3 vols.

Parkman, Francis. *Pioneers of France in the New World.* Boston, 1897, 2 vols. — Full title.

———. *Montcalm and Wolf.* Boston, 1897, 3 vols.

———. *The Jesuits in North America.* Boston, 1897, 2 vols. — Full title.

———. *The Old Régime in Canada.* Boston, 1897, 2 vols. — Parkman, *Old Régime.*

———. *The Old Régime in Canada.* Boston, 1874. — Parkman, *Old Régime.*

Report of the Statistics of the Bureau of Labor, Mass., 1882. "The Canadian-French in New England." Boston, 1882.

Reyss, Paul. *Etude sur quelques points de l'histoire de tolérance au Canada et aux Antilles.* Génève, 1907.

Robinson, J. H. *Introduction to the History of Western Europe.* Boston, 1903.

Royal Society of Canada. *Proceedings and Transactions.* 1900.

———. *Proceedings and Transactions.* Ottawa, 1905.

Ruffini, Francesco. *Religious Liberty.* New York, 1912.

Salone, Emile. *Le colonisation de la Nouvelle-France.* Paris, 1905. Salone.

Siegfried, André. *Le Canada, les deux races, problèmes politiques contemporains.* Paris, 1906.

Smith, R. Travers. *The Church in France.* New York, 1912.

Sulte, Benjamin. *The Origins of the French Canadians* (in *Proceedings and Transactions of the Royal Society of Canada,* 1905). Ottawa, 1906. Sulte.

Têtu, Henri. *Les Évêques de Québec.* Québec, 1889.

ERRATA

PAGE

25. For "botanist" read "Swedish naturalist".

76, 144 and 156. For "Maseres" read "Masères".

78, 81, 83, 84 and 85. For "Mémoires sur le Canada" read "Nouvelles Acquisitions Françaises 9273".

136. For "ministers" read "minister", for "they" "he", and for "them" "him".

136 and 137. For "M. de Ramsey" read "M. de Ramsay".

138. For "to be afforded" read "were to be afforded".

145. For "ladys" read "ladies", and for "effect" "affect".

146. For "conquerer" read "conqueror", and on pp. 146, 149 and 154, for "Cramahe", "Cramhé", "Cramaché" respectively read "Cramahé".

147. For "Superior Council" read "Sovereign Council".

149. For "lesson" read "lessen".

150. For "Haldemand" read "Haldimand" and for "De la Valiniere" read "De la Valinière".

153. For "this opinion" read "This is an opinion".

157. "Hold, receive . . . said Religion", "the religious Orders . . . excepted", "to hold . . . Civil Rights" should be enclosed in quotation marks.

160. For "beneficient" read "beneficent".

VITA

WALTER ALEXANDER RIDDELL was born at Stratford, in the Province of Ontario, Canada, on the fifth of August 1881. His elementary and secondary education was received in the schools of Denver, Colorado, and Manitoba, Canada. He was matriculated in the University of Manitoba from Manitoba College in 1903, received the degree of B. A. from the former institution in 1907, the degree of A. M. (in Sociology) from Columbia University in 1908, and the degree of B. D. from Union Theological Seminary in 1912. During the summer of 1912 he worked under the direction of Dr. Warren H. Wilson, Superintendent of the Department of Church and Country Life of the Board of Home Missions of the Presbyterian Church of the United States, in the Ohio Rural Life Survey. During the fall of 1912 and during the greater part of 1913 he made researches for his dissertation, in the archives of London, Paris and Ottawa. From June to September, 1913, he studied in Ottawa as " Research Fellow from the University of Manitoba in Canadian Archives." In the fall of that year he was appointed director of social surveys for the Methodist and Presbyterian churches in Canada, a position which he still holds. In Columbia University he studied under Professors Giddings, Tenney, Chaddock, Seager, McGiffert and Rockwell, and attended the seminars of Professor Giddings and of Professor McGiffert.